GREEN NETWORKS OF THE
DALES
TWENTY MAGNIFICENT LINEAR WALKS

GREEN NETWORKS OF THE
DALES
TWENTY MAGNIFICENT LINEAR WALKS

Colin Speakman

GREAT NORTHERN

For all those dedicated campaigners of the Yorkshire Dales Society, Ramblers Association, CPRE, YHA, Friends of the Settle-Carlisle Line, Friends of Dales Rail, and Yorkshire Dales Public Transport Users Group without whose constant effort and vigilance this book would not have been possible.

And for Fleur who shared the bus journeys, the pathfinding and the walks.

Thanks too to the Yorkshire Dales National Park Ranger Service and the Nidderdale Rangers who have done and are doing such excellent work on footpaths and access areas.

Great Northern Books
PO Box 213, Ilkley, LS29 9WS

© Text and photographs, Colin Speakman 2006
© Maps, Harvey Map Services Ltd, Doune, Perthshire, 2006
Front cover photograph (near Malham): © Rod Edwards / Alamy

ISBN: 1 905080 15 8

Design and layout: Richard Joy

Printed by Quebecor Ibérica, Barcelona

British Cataloguing in Publication Data
A catalogue for this book is available from the British Library

Contents

Foreword (by Mike Harding)   7

The Green Networks of the Yorkshire Dales   10

Practical Points   17

Useful organisations   20

THE WALKS

1. **Rombald's Way:** Otley - Ilkey - Addingham - Skipton   21

2. **Between Two Spas:** Ilkley - Harrogate   26

3. **Sharp Haw and Elbolton:** Skipton - Grassington   30

4. **Grimwith and Stump Cross:** Grassington - Pateley Bridge   34

5. **The Washburn Way:** Otley - Blubberhouses - Pateley Bridge   38

6. **The Fountains Walk:** Pateley Bridge - Brimham Rocks -
    Fountains Abbey - Ripon   43

7. **Across the Nidderdale Watershed:** Kilnsey - Pateley Bridge   48

8. **Over the Stake Pass:** Buckden - Semerwater - Hawes   53

9. **The Old Kendal Road:** Skipton - Settle   57

10. **Along the Craven Fault:** Settle - Malham - Grassington   61

11. **Malham Tarn and the Monk's Road:** Hellifield - Malham - Buckden 66

12. **Walden:** Kettlewell - Aysgarth   71

13. **Crummackdale and Ingleborough:** Settle - Ingleton   76

14. **The Whernside Ridge:** Ingleton - Dentdale   80

15. **Wild Boar Fell:** Garsdale - Kirkby Stephen   84

16. **Lady Anne's Way:** Hawes (Garsdale) - Kirkby Stephen   88

17. **Over Apedale:** Leyburn - Redmire - Bolton Castle - Reeth   94

18. **The Wensleydale Walk:** Hawes - Askrigg - Bolton Castle - Redmire 98

19. **Upper Swaledale:** Keld - Gunnerside - Reeth   103

20. **Marrick Priory and Willance's Leap:** Reeth - Marske - Richmond 108

(Above) Walkers on Walden Road – an ancient packhorse way *(Walk 12)*.
(Page 1) Dentdale from the Craven Way *(Walk 14)*.
(Pages 2-3) Summit cairns, Wild Boar Fell *(Walk 15)*.

Foreword

We're lucky in this country in that, just before it was too late, men of vision saw that the great maw of industry which had already destroyed so much – turning some of the best land in the world into the Black Country and turning Manchester from a mediaeval village into one of the busiest and most important cities on the planet – would, if it were allowed to go on, trash whatever was left of this island. The National Parks, our lungs and our spiritual open air cathedrals, are the result of the work of people like John Dower, Arthur Raistrick and Tom Stephenson, men who saw that the only way to save what was left of the wild places was to protect and conserve them.

I've spent some of the best days of my life in the Parks, walking, cycling, taking my children for picnics, playing music in the pubs, photographing them and writing about them and I love them no less now than I did when I first started climbing and walking as a teenager from the smoky streets of Manchester.

The Yorkshire Dales are my great love, there is nowhere on earth like them, and over the years I've walked most of the paths and bridleways and trespassed a bit too – though without criminal intent. One of the things I always meant to do was put together a book of linear walks so that, instead of having to walk in a circle back to where I'd left the car, I could get trains or buses back to where I started. Now Colin Speakman has saved me the trouble, and a fine book it is too.

You can do these walks as day walks or you can link them together in all kinds of permutations. I particularly like the idea of linking a few of them together starting and finishing at stations on the Settle-Carlisle line and yet taking in further flung villages where there are good pubs that do bed and breakfast – how people used to ramble before the car came along to convince us that without it we were lost and damned. I've been meaning to spend a few days walking from village to village with some old friends, meeting up in Settle and then setting out to wander, following old green lanes and highways, seeing where the journey might take us – and this is just the book for such an aimless and yet deliciously purposeful project.

Mike Harding
President, Yorkshire Dales Society

ROUTE & TRAVEL MAP

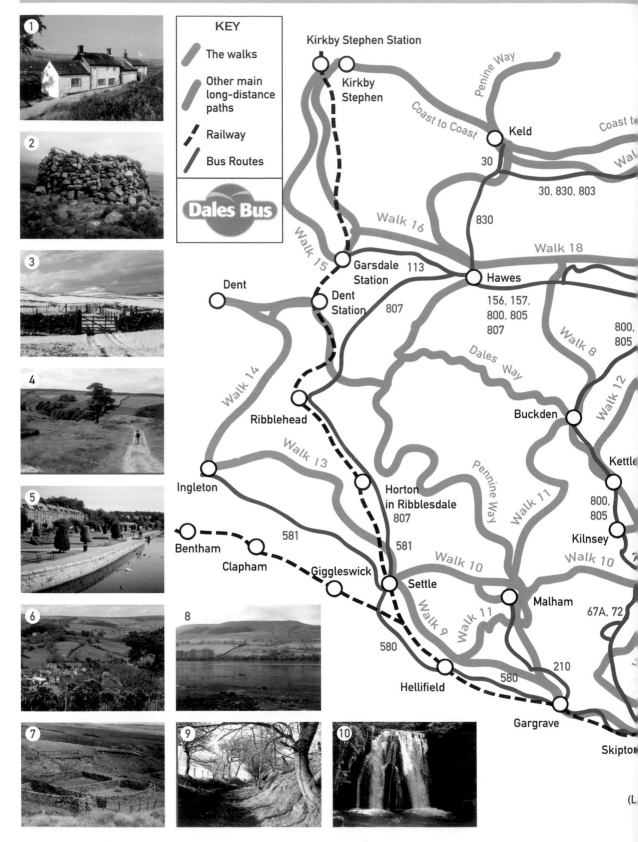

KEY

The walks

Other main long-distance paths

Railway

Bus Routes

Dales Bus

Kirkby Stephen Station

Kirkby Stephen

Penine Way

Coast to Coast

Keld

Coast to

Wal

30

30, 830, 803

830

Walk 16

Walk 18

Dent

Walk 15

Garsdale Station

113

Hawes

Dent Station

807

156, 157, 800, 805 807

800, 805

Walk 8

Walk 14

Ribblehead

Dales Way

Buckden

Walk 12

Kettle

Walk 13

Horton in Ribblesdale

807

Pennine Way

Walk 11

800, 805

Ingleton

581

581

Kilnsey

Walk 10

Walk 10

Bentham

581

Walk 10

Clapham

Giggleswick

Settle

Walk 9

Walk 11

Malham

67A, 72

580

210

Hellifield

580

Gargrave

Skipton

(L

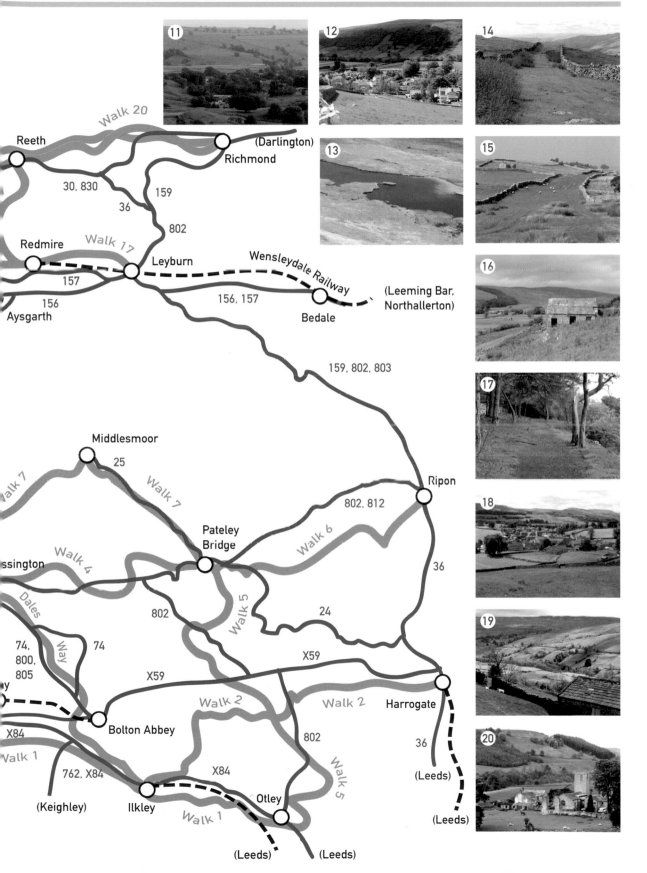

Reeth

Walk 20

(Darlington)
Richmond

30, 830

159

36

802

Redmire

Walk 17

Leyburn

Wensleydale Railway

157

156, 157

(Leeming Bar,
Northallerton)

156

Aysgarth

Bedale

159, 802, 803

Middlesmoor

25

Walk 7

alk 7

Ripon

Walk 6

802, 812

Pateley
Bridge

36

ssington

Walk 4

Walk 5

24

Dales

802

Way

74,
800,
805

74

X59

X59

Walk 2

Walk 2

Harrogate

ay

X84

Bolton Abbey

802

36

Walk 1

X84

Walk 5

(Leeds)

762, X84

(Keighley)

Ilkley

Otley

(Leeds)

Walk 1

(Leeds)

(Leeds)

11

12

14

13

15

16

17

18

19

20

INTRODUCTION

The Green Networks of the Yorkshire Dales

This is a very different kind of book about walking in the Yorkshire Dales. It sets out what might be described as a radical, even controversial theory about countryside walking.

It suggests that to truly experience the richness, vastness and complexity of a great landscape such as the Yorkshire Dales it is necessary to change that close physical, almost symbiotic relationship most visitors to the Dales, including walkers, have with their own car.

If you look at the pattern of most popular leisure walks undertaken in the Yorkshire Dales in the early twenty-first century, and these are traced out on a map, you'd see a dense series of circles, jagged and elongated, mostly about three to eight miles in length, the lines especially thick and dense around popular National Park and village car parks. It's easy to see why. There are literally scores of guidebooks, of every shape and size, describing circular walks in the Yorkshire Dales. There are family walks, pub walks, tea-shop walks, waterfall walks, most of them replicating yet again the same familiar walks, almost all between three and eight miles in length, so that once hidden and forgotten paths are now a couple of metres wide and on a fine Sunday afternoon you'll invariably see someone in front of you, book open at page eight, muttering about turning right at the next gate.

It is excellent that this should be so. More people than ever before are out walking in the Dales not because they have to, but because of the delight and pleasures of countryside walking and the many physical and mental benefits that regular outdoor exercise brings. But the very

first sentence of almost every walk description begins with the words 'Park at...' It has even been suggested that the most important piece of equipment for a rambler is not a decent pair of boots, but a shiny, sleek motor car capable of taking you in what is usually a matter of minutes from your front doorstep to the place to park at the start of a walk.

Too bad if you don't own a car or don't drive. Very few guidebook writers will bother to tell you that you can in fact almost always get to the start of a walk by bus or train. This is despite the fact that around a quarter of the population live in households that don't have a car, and even more don't have access to a car if it is in use by another member of the household – a partner or parent – or you don't have a driving licence. In any other field of activity, such discrimination against a large minority of the population would be severely censured – and rightly so.

Yet even if you can get to the start of the walk on a bus, you're still having to do a walk which is designed specially for motorists – a circular walk designed to bring the walker back safely to the security of the parked vehicle.

This is actually a huge constraint, a contradiction of the alleged 'freedom' of the car, acting almost like an invisible umbilical cord that attaches you, physically and physiologically, to that little piece of your home on wheels. Getting back to the security of your car becomes a very necessary part of the day out.

That's where the Green Networks of the Dales come in.

Up to the middle of last century, for most

people in Britain (as it still is in many parts of the world) walking was their prime form of transport, often the only available or affordable form of travelling between villages, from villages into towns, even between towns. Many of the paths and tracks we use as part of a circular, leisure walk include sections of older, longer routes. Such routes were used at least from medieval times and well into the railway and motorbus age, as the only way of getting around. Our ancestors thought nothing of walking a dozen miles to and from a market town or to visit their friends. Two or three hours vigorous walking to get to where you wanted to be, to work, to worship or to visit a relative, was a normal human activity. Only the wealthy rode on horseback, or took a coach on what until the middle of the 18th century were rough, often impassable roads. In areas such as the Pennines, where roads were especially bad, the packhorse train was the only way in which raw materials such as wool, coal, or finished goods, could be carried from or between Dales villages or townships.

Nobody suggests going back to the age before mechanised transport. But to rediscover, on foot, the many ancient linear routes used by our ancestors, which in many cases have changed little over the centuries, is a magnificent way of beginning to understand that landscape, the settlement and land use patterns, the relationship of villages with their market towns. Such routes in ancient times avoided the swamp infested, densely forested valley floors, but even in later years were the most direct way for human or animal muscle power. They can still be traced, following the higher slopes of every Yorkshire dale, moorland or mountain passes, linking daleheads along tracks which retain their grass-covered or crudely cobbled surfaces, little changed since the days when packhorses carried produce to market or river port.

To walk such routes away from modern tarmac roads with their incessant roar of traffic, fumes and physical threat, is to inhabit that older, slower world. The frantic, destructive pace of modern living has created a kind of hyper-mobility, an obsessive pattern of behaviour, so that driving from place to place, usually at high speed, almost becomes an end in itself. We are always going places – but ultimately may have nowhere to go. Modern transport both shrinks and diminishes the world.

Rediscovering the sheer size, complexity and scale of the landscape, taking perhaps a whole day to walk a dozen or so miles that, on tarmac, takes around twenty minutes in a car, is a joy in itself. It is a totally different way of perceiving that landscape.

A start is to break the tyranny of the motor vehicle by escaping its demands for circular walks. The Germans have a word 'Zielwanderung', literally walking with a destination or purpose, point-to-point, as indeed all walking activity used to be. Perhaps we need a Campaign for Real Walks, for walks that are actually going somewhere.

A destination is therefore the essence of all longer distance walking. The great, ever popular long distance walks of the Dales the Pennine Way, the Dales Way, the Coast to Coast – share this element of having a purpose, whether it is to the Scottish border, the Lake District or the coastal cliffs of Yorkshire. That's part of their magic, as is staying overnight in a dales village, whether farmhouse, village inn or youth hostel, meeting local people and contributing, with what you spend, to the local economy. At last long distance walking is being recognised as perhaps the most important form of sustainable tourism, that is tourism causing least damage to the environment whilst delivering maximum benefit to the local economy.

This book is about exactly that kind of experience. It suggests a series of twenty middle distance linear walks in the Yorkshire Dales with a purpose, which are deliberately selected to tie in with towns or larger villages with services and facilities, where by spending money on those services you are also helping the local economy. They also tie in with good quality public transport. This means that that they can, in most cases, be done as day walks, though in some cases you need to have a long summer day available.

There's no need to be put off by the length of the walks. They have almost all been deliberately designed to be split into comfortable, shorter day 'Stages', especially valuable on short winter days, when you are more likely to run out of daylight than energy. Each intermediate or 'Stage Point'described in the text has convenient available return buses or trains to allow you to split the walk into half or even a third to spread it over a couple or more days,. Alternatively they can be reduced to half day walks, for example in the winter months. Doing what our ancestors also did – staying overnight at your destination or even part way along at or close to one of the Staging Points - enables the walk to be part of a weekend or short walking holiday trip and makes your experience even more interesting and rewarding. And by so doing you contribute more to the local economy whilst making minimal environmental impact – true sustainable tourism.

For this reason, most of the walks also easily access the network of modern, comfortable Youth Hostels in the Yorkshire Dales, or where there isn't a hostel, Dales market towns and larger villages where there is a good choice of overnight accommodation, bed and breakfast, inns or small hotels – and sometimes camp sites. Because the walks all end close to a rail station or bus stop, there is likely to be a well timed late afternoon or early evening bus or train to take you to that accommodation, or if you are on a day trip, quickly and easily back to where you live.

If a car has to be used for all or part of your journey (and the logistics of using public transport all the way from home even to the edge of the Dales are sometimes formidable), then suggestions are made of where you can leave your vehicle safely and securely at least for a day and take a bus or train to access one or both ends of the walk.

The real advantage of not being restricted to circular walks from car parks is that many fine walks can be included which as far as this author is aware have never before appeared in print – because they are not circular car walks. However, whilst I have deliberately avoided using already well known and well established routes such as the Pennine Way and Dales Way, sections of some established long distance routes are included because they fit the criteria for good public transport links and with a choice of overnight accommodation. I have also incorporated some sections of the Nidderdale Way into two routes in Nidderdale, partly because it is a very fine walk in its own right which deserves to be better known, but also because it offers a high quality waymarked and well maintained route through the Nidderdale Area of Outstanding Natural Beauty in an area where otherwise there can be problems. The same is true of part of the Harrogate Dales Way link between Fewston and Harrogate.

What emerges from the twenty routes is a network of cross-Dales routes, all middle distance, that is between twelve and twenty-two miles in length. Together with the established long distance trails, these form a superb Green Network, a walker's grid across and through the Dales. They link the main market towns and larger villages, thereby tying the routes in firmly with that other Green Network of the Dales – the increasingly good quality, and in most cases, moderately frequent public transport services. This means that if one bus or train is missed there is usually another in an hour or so. It is also possible to combine walks or use convenient link paths at appropriate points to create wider route choice as the whim takes you – true flexibility and freedom denied the motorist. Or you could combine several walks, end to end, over several days, to create a remarkable series of cross-Dales walks, for example from Otley to Ingleton or Dent, from Hellifield to Kirkby Stephen, from Skipton to Reeth, from Settle to Ripon.

This Green Network, which offers infinite choice and flexibility for the public-transport literate walker, reclaims the Yorkshire Dales from the monopoly of the motor car, offering an alter-

Elaine's Teas - Local enterprise near Reeth provides sustenance for Coast to Coast and other Dales walkers. (Walk 20)

native, far richer and more rewarding way to experience the Dales. Linear walking also turns on its head the ultimate irony of twenty-first century mass mechanised transport and much pre-packaged destination marketing. As well as threatening the whole future of human civilisation by its contribution to global warming, mechanised travel effectively destroys both time and space, as in reality we spend more and more time travelling ever longer distances along ever more crowded roads, with eventually nowhere left to travel to of real interest.

Walking the Dales, and taking maybe several days to do so, will enable you to recapture that time and space – and a very special sense of place. And in truth, these are walks for connoisseurs, longer, perhaps tougher than the average car ramble, designed for serious, experienced walkers, who can read and interpret a map. Hopefully such walks will enable you to share and explore something that is quintessential about the Yorkshire Dales, a special quality that makes it a walker's landscape without equal.

What makes the Yorkshire Dales so special for walkers?

Most of the Yorkshire Dales, that part of the Central Pennines of England between the Aire and Stainmore Gaps, is protected landscape, either within the Yorkshire Dales National Park, which extends from Bolton Abbey to the Howgill Fells in Cumbria, or the more recently established Nidderdale Area of Outstanding Natural Beauty that covers the eastern Dales from Washburndale and Nidderdale to Colsterdale.

What makes the Dales such a wonderful landscape and such a marvellous place for walkers is that rare harmony between human activity and the natural world – the cultural landscape. When you walk in the Dales you are aware of that stark contrast between the bare, brown, almost austere moorland sum-

Washdub Bridge, Crummackdale, typical of many similar delightful corners in the Dales. (Walk 13)

mits, covered by peat, heather, rushes and cotton grass, their very barrenness a result of human activity, and the fertile, green, sheltered valleys or dales that penetrate deep into the hills. The intimate patterns of drystone walls, scattered barns and woodlands create an archetypical northern English landscape, nowhere better to be seen than in the Yorkshire Dales. The grey stone walls, farmhouses and villages, built out of local stone, seem to have grown out of the very bedrock itself, identical in colour and texture to the outcropping crags and scars on the moorland edge above.

Becks tumble down the steep, often glaciated valley sides creating at times spectacular waterfalls, and deep, hidden gills, usually overhung with rowan trees with their scarlet berries in August, and each crevice with a scattering of primroses in spring. These are places frequented only by shepherds and walkers, the silence broken by the sharp cry of curlew, plover and sigh of the wind across the moorland grass, forming a background to the visual splendours of the open dale.

Human activity is not only evident in the landscape in terms of ancient settlement and land-use patterns, dating back to Bronze Age times, with a strong monastic influence as the great sheep walks of the higher Dales were laid out from the twelfth century onwards, but also in industrial activity, with the huge impact of lead mining. This peaked in the late eighteenth and early nineteenth centuries, leaving major industrial scars across the upland landscape which, over a century and a half since the industry collapsed, have mellowed into the fascinating moorland industrial archaeology of the upper Dales.

Equally much of the Dales since Norman and Plantagenet times, has always been a leisure landscape, with great, protected areas of medieval hunting 'Forests' or Chases. These in turn were replaced by the great estates and parkland of the eighteenth and nineteenth centuries, with huge areas protected and managed as heather moorland for grouse shooting.

To the south and west of the Dales is the limestone country, the huge scars and crags of Carboniferous or Mountain Limestone which, along several major fault lines, is exposed and weathered to create such dramatic natural features as Malham Cove, Gordale Scar and Attermire above Settle, as well as an immense network of caves and potholes that attracts potholers from all over Britain. About half of all the limestone pavement in the British Isles is to be found in the Yorkshire Dales. In the Spring months, the woods and meadows, especially in the northern dales such as Swaledale, are rich with the colour and scent of wildflowers, with old herb-rich meadows one of the defining features of the upper dale.

However this is also largely a farmed landscape, with Dales farmers, and to a lesser extent foresters, having to earn a living from the land as producers of milk, meat, wool and timber, with hill sheep and cattle dominating upland pastures and moorland grazing. Unlike much of lowland Britain where prairie type arable farms have largely obliterated the historic landscape, there is a cultural and visual continuity in the Dales. Increasingly, however, farmers have to manage that landscape in ways that help to protect its special qualities.

Farmers are the true guardians of the Dales landscape heritage. Increasingly the Yorkshire Dales National Park Authority and Nidderdale AONB Joint Advisory Committee, in partnerships with such agencies as Natural England (English Nature), English Heritage, the Environment Agencies, DEFRA and the Yorkshire Dales Millennium Trust, are working closely with farmers and landowners. A variety of schemes now support the work of farmers and land managers to help protect natural biodiversity and landscape heritage.

By respecting the life and work of the farming community, by keeping to paths and trails on all enclosed land, by closing all gates (unless when they are clearly propped open), by never climbing drystone walls, by walking single file across the lush grass of spring meadows, and above all keeping dogs on leads wherever there is livestock or where birds are breeding (especially important in spring time), walkers will always be welcome in the Dales countryside.

This is a highly accessible landscape. Throughout the whole area is a remarkable network of public footpaths and bridleways, historic routes between villages, to and from the village church, between villages and the market town, across and between the heads of dales. These are recorded on County Council Definitive Maps which are legal documents, used by publishers such as Harvey or the Ordnance Survey to give walkers confirmation that a legal right of way exists.

Not all access is universally welcome. One category of right of way is Byways Open to All Traffic. These are often precisely the ancient, unsurfaced green ways of the Dales described and used for walks in this book. They were long distance packhorse or drovers' routes over the high fells. The threats come from a new generation of motorised users, drivers of all-terrain 4x4 vehicles and motor cycles, who see driving these ancient routes as a challenge sport. In so doing, on certain routes they inflict grievous damage to their historic surfaces, as well as destroying the peace and tranquillity for local residents and other visitors. The roar of their engines, sometimes with their silencers deliberately modified for maximum impact, can literally fill a valley with intrusive noise.

Controlling this threat to the integrity of both the National Park and AONB is now a major challenge to the authorities, faced as they are with well organised pressure groups who use in effect what is currently a loophole in the law. This allows useage of tracks by horse- drawn carts in the remote past as a legal

proof that they can now be used by modern, heavyweight motor vehicles.

This is just one of the many challenges faced by the National Park Authority and the AONB Joint Advisory Committee, who both have to deal with the problems of controlling building development, so that new building fits in with nationally important landscapes. At the same time they have to seek ways of ensuring that visitors do not destroy, with their activities, the very countryside and natural environment they most value.

Because National Parks have a prime function of facilitating and encouraging appropri-

Janet's Foss Wood, a delightful stretch of walking between Malham and Gordale Scar. (Walk 10)

ate forms of public enjoyment, the Yorkshire Dales National Park is far better resourced than the Nidderdale AONB. As well as providing welcoming and informative Visitor Centres, the standard of maintenance and way marking of footpaths and bridlepaths is generally higher. But there is an excellent, seemingly infinite choice of wonderful walking routes through both protected areas, only a fraction of which can be suggested in this book.

Practical Points

This book is not intended to be a field guide. It is neither the size nor the shape to fit into a rucksack pocket. It is intended to suggest some of the best available routes, to enthuse and inspire the discovery of twenty especially fine linear walking routes through the Yorkshire Dales. It is intended to help pre-plan walks before a visit. Actual route finding must rely on the only really useful, practical tool available to you on the ground, a decent footpath map.

In terms of route finding, words are vague tools and can easily be misinterpreted, especially when landmarks such as signing, buildings or gates or even walls and fences change. By translating the route from the descriptive text onto the map before the walk, path finding - which can be fun – is relatively easy. The map can also allow variations to meet your own circumstances including weather conditions and return transport.

Most footpaths and bridleways in the Yorkshire Dales now have the standard yellow or blue waymarks, and are signed where they leave public roads. However signs and waymarks are often absent, and good map reading and pathfinding is essential.

Harvey Maps of Doune, Perthshire, are partners in this guidebook, and we have no hesitation in strongly recommending their series of excellent maps, produced from detailed recent aerial survey, at 1:40,000 scale, which show rights of way clearly, as well as field walls, which are often essential for route finding. The four key walking maps, Dales East, North, South and West respectively, are identified with each walk. However, if you prefer to have even greater detail then the OS Explorer 1:25,000 series maps are also recommended to augment your Harvey map, and for small sections of some walks which are not currently on a Harvey map.

The publication of this book coincides with the publication of Access to Open Country Maps of the Yorkshire Dales, which have been drawn up as a result of the CROW Act 2000. Around 62% of the Yorkshire Dales National Park and 34% of Nidderdale AONB are now officially recognised as areas of unenclosed moorland, common or heath which are open to the public on foot. Though most of the suggested routes use long established public rights of way (or in some cases long recognised permissive routes), sections have been included which cross these new Public Access Areas. In exceptional circumstances, such as times of high fire risk or on shooting days, they could be closed to public access. There are also restrictions concerning dogs, which usually have to be kept on a lead, but in other cases, for example over grouse moors, they may be totally banned except where there are rights of way. In almost every case, alternative paths or lanes are available to avoid such problems.

Details of the new Access Areas, and further information about the Yorkshire Dales National Park, including local accommodation, can be obtained from National Park Centres or via the National Park web site on www.yorkshiredales.org.uk., whilst information about Nidderdale AONB is available on www.nidderdaleaonb.org.uk. Further information about new access rights in the English countryside is available on www.countrysideaccess.gov.uk.

Public transport, contrary to popular mythology, has improved dramatically to and within the Dales over the last decade. There are very frequent suburban train services from Leeds and Bradford to Ilkley, Skipton and Harrogate, and regular services along the Leeds-Settle-Carlisle line, seven days a week. Local Dales bus services have improved beyond recognition, with the excellent Dales Bus summer weekend network supplementing hourly or at minimum two hourly weekday local bus services along most of the major dales. These services facilitate a huge choice of linear walks. It is worth bearing in mind that when choosing to use a bus or train, you are not just helping to save the environment from local and global pollution. You are also contributing important extra revenue to bus and train services in the Dales which local communities depend on – a double benefit that should be supported by everyone who truly cares for the Dales.

The Arriva 805 bus service to Hawes, photographed at Grassington.

Metro (West Yorkshire PTE), North Yorkshire County Council and Cumbria County Council offer booklets and local timetables which contain both comprehensive bus and local rail services, and up to the minute information can also be obtained by using one of two excellent web sites. These are the outstanding Dales Bus web site, created by the Yorkshire Dales Public Transport Users Group on www.dalesbus.org and the Travel Dales site organised by the local authorities on www.traveldales.org.uk. This last also has details of the Dales Bus discount scheme where bus and train users get useful discounts from local tourist businesses in the Dales. Make sure you check out the range of available bargain bus and train tickets currently available – with or without rail cards or bus passes, so you keep travel costs to a minimum. In addition the national Traveline phone service, operated 8am to 8pm daily on 0870 608 2608, will give local bus service and rail information anywhere in the UK including the Yorkshire Dales, for the price of a local call.

If you enjoy walking with others, the

A party of walkers leave the Settle-Carlisle train at Dent station.

Yorkshire Dales Public Transport Users Group organises weekly linear walks, all year, on public transport from West Yorkshire using Dales Bus services (details on the web site above). There are similar weekly walks from the Settle-Carlisle and Leeds-Morecambe line trains organised by the Friends of Dales Rail and the Friends of the Settle-Carlisle Line.

As well as good maps, a compass and a timetable, it is essential always to take warm clothing and fully protective rainwear with you in a comfortable, waterproof rucksack, whenever walking in the Dales. Even in the height of summer, Pennine weather is notoriously fickle and conditions on northern hills can be as severe as anywhere in Britain – especially in wind and rain. Boots, at least of the lightweight variety, are essential on all these walks, and many people find walking sticks or poles a valuable aid, especially when steep descents have to be faced.

Always carry sufficient food and water with you. Even if you are planning a pub lunch, make sure you have at least a litre of water and some high energy emergency rations such as chocolate or dates. Hypothermia, caused by tiredness and exposure to the elements without sufficient food or protective clothing, can be fatal. A small first aid outfit is also strongly advisable.

Many people also believe a mobile phone is now essential, especially when walking alone—but many places in the Dales can be out of phone range and the prime need is to be well equipped when out on the fells, and to keep within your physical limits and those imposed by current weather conditions. Common sense is the best security system of all, including, if walking alone, letting a relative or friend know where you are going and when you are likely to arrive.

A good linear walk is a bit like a story that unfolds through time and space as you walk. Like all good stories, it has to have a beginning, a middle and an end, so that you know you have arrived somewhere, the walk's is purpose fulfilled, with time to find that café or pub, to relax before seeking overnight accommodation or your return travel. A good walk needs to have some real highlights, some visual moments or historic features that make it memorable. Inevitably the 20 walks in this book are a personal, individual choice. But one thing they all have in common is that they all have a purpose, a destination, offering the sense of achievement when you reach your destination that all good walks need.

Enjoy them!

SOME USEFUL CONTACTS

Campaign to Protect Rural England (CPRE)
128 Southwark Street
London SE1 0SW
Tel 020 7981
www.cpre.nrg.uk

Ramblers' Association
2nd Floor, Camelford House
87-90 Albert Embankment
London
SE1 7TW
Tel 020 7339 8500
www.ramblers.org.uk

Nidderdale AONB
Council Offices
King Street
Pateley Bridge
Harrogate
HG3 5LE
Tel 01423 712950
www.nidderdale.co.uk

Open Spaces Society
25a Bell Street
Henley-on-Thames
Oxfordshire
RG9 2BA
www.oss.org.uk

Friends of Dales Rail
35 Wancliffe Drive
Leeds
LS11 8ET
www.friendsofdalesrail.org

Friends of the Settle-Carlisle Line
14 Springfield Lane
Morley
Leeds
LS27 9PH
www.settle-carlisle.org

Yorkshire Dales Public Transport Users Group
29 Somerville
Peterborough
PE4 5BB
www.dalesbus.org

Yorkshire Dales National Park Authority (Visitor Services)
Colvend
Hebden Road
Grassington
North Yorkshire
BD23 5LB
01756 752748
www.yorkshiredales.org.uk

Yorkshire Dales Society
The Civic Centre,
Cross Green
Otley
West Yorkshire
LS21 1HD
Tel 01943 461938
www.yds.org.uk

Youth Hostels Association
Trevelyan House
Dimple Road
Matlock
Derbyshire
DE4 3YH
Tel 01629 592600
www.yha.org.uk

Rombald's Way

OTLEY TO SKIPTON

Rombald's Moor is the name given to that massive area of Pennine gritstone upland that divides Airedale and Wharfedale, rising to rising to 402 metres or 1,321 feet and forming a major feature of the central Pennines. For millennia the river valleys, running north-west to south-east, which skirt the moorland have formed a natural pass through the Pennines, the so-called Aire Gap, used by road, canal and railway. Far

older, perhaps, is the Aire-Wharfe gap, the relatively low pass through the Pennines which in prehistoric times was undoubtedly a trade route from Ireland to the rivers leading to the East Coast, including a Roman Road linking forts at Ribchester, Elslack, Ilkley, Tadcaster and York. Many of these ancient pre-turnpike highways remain as minor roads, tracks and even footpaths. The incredibly rich archaeological remains to be found along the moorland edges have led one local historian, the late Eric Cowling, to claim an ancient trans-Pennine route, Rombald's Way.

This high-level, moorland edge walk, linking the modern towns of Otley, Ilkley and Skipton, follows much of Cowling's suggested route and includes part of Ilkley Moor, Yorkshire's most famous and best loved area of open moorland. The route can be completed on a long summer day as a single 18-mile hike, or divided into easier stages making full use of the frequent X84 Leeds-Otley-Ilkley-Skipton bus service which parallels this walk along the main valley roads between the town centres.

FACT FILE

Distance: 18 miles (28 kilometres).

Terrain: Some steep ascents onto the high moorland then a mixture of woodland and moorland paths and tracks, some sections of field paths and a short section of urban walking.

Refreshment and Accommodation: Menston Arms, Menston. Hermit Inn, Burley Woodhead – open daily, lunchtimes, food. Cow and Calf Hotel, Ilkley daily, all day. White Wells, Ilkley – light refreshments (weekends and holiday times only). Wide choice of inns and cafes in Ilkley, Addingham, Skipton.

Toilets: Otley, Ilkley, Addingham, Skipton.

Transport: Outward: X84 bus from Leeds to Otley, Ilkley, Addingham, Skipton – every 20/30 minutes to Ilkley. Return: Frequent train and bus services to Leeds, X84 to Ilkley, Otley.

Stage points: Menston (3 miles/5km – Metrotrain); Ilkley (8 miles/13km), X84 to Otley, Leeds, Metrotrain to Leeds and Bradford; Addingham (12.5/20km miles), X84 to Ilkley, Otley, Leeds.

Drivers: Park Otley or Ilkley (extensive public car parks) and use service X84.

Route

Otley is a compact market town, rich in character, and notable for its busy market place, ancient yards and courts, choice of shops and pubs, and delightful riverside area. It is dominated to the south by the huge bulk of The Chevin, which is the first major feature on the walk.

The walk starts from the bus station, turning right into Bondgate past the fire station and left into Station Road (before the parish

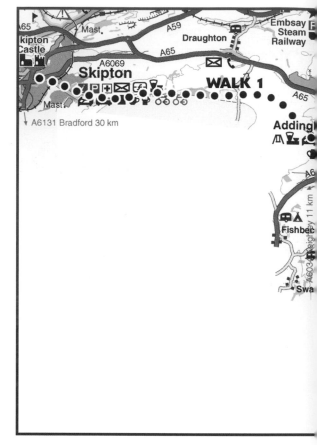

Guidestoop near Chelker – a seventeenth century guidepost and waymark at the junction of old roads to Skipton and Silsden.

church). At the end of this road, by the cobbled station yard that is the last relic of the former railway station, a footbridge leads to an enclosed path past smallholdings and Victorian terraced housing into Chevin Forest Park.

The Chevin, an area of gritstone outcrop high above Wharfedale which forms an outlier of the Pennines, takes it name from the Celtic word for crag. Much of this Danefield Estate was given to the people of Otley by Major Horton-Fawkes, a local landowner, as a permanent memorial to those who died in the two World Wars. It now forms the centrepiece of the Chevin Forest Park.

The enclosed way becomes a cobbled and then steeply stepped path through attractive beech woods, with increasingly superb views

as compensation for the climb. Allow time to pause and enjoy these views. As you emerge from the wood onto open heath either continue in a straight line up the steep hillside ahead, or take the gentler path to the left, zigzagging up to the summit 'Surprise View'. A little disappointingly for those who have climbed on foot, this has a busy car park.

The view is breathtaking. A viewfinder to the left indicates the whereabouts of York Minster and the White Horse of Kilburn on a clear day. On most days there is a splendid panorama across Otley with its green backcloth of the Washburn Valley and Nidderdale AONB, with Almscliffe Crag featuring to the east. There is also a fine view to the south, back into Airedale, with Leeds-Bradford airport just over the horizon.

Follow the path westwards that goes along the summit ridge before entering the beech woods and reaching the end of The Chevin. A

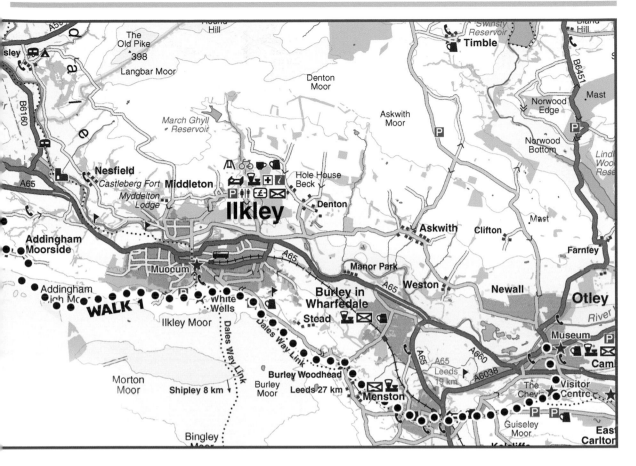

stile gives access onto York Gate, the line of the Roman Road, but now a busy short cut for speeding motorists between Airedale and north Leeds. Left at the junction, first right to Chevin Inn, behind which a field path leads past Chevin End Farm. Follow the Dales Way link waymarks across a field to a tarmac drive, left and first right along a path that follows the railway to the A65. Cross with care and follow the road ahead to Menston station.

Head for the platform but at the footbridge take the narrow enclosed way between high garden fences that leads to a road junction. Take Fairfax Way directly ahead until a T-junction where you turn left onto Main Street then right, continuing straight ahead along Bleach Mill Lane as the main road bears left.

This soon leaves urban Menston behind and becomes a narrow unsurfaced lane with fine views across the Wharfe valley. Keep ahead past Bleach Mill Cottages and Hag Wood Farm, always keeping the same direction until the path reaches the main road at Burley Woodhead – the Hermit Inn if required is to your left.

Otherwise cross the main road, keeping right until, on the left, a gate and signpost indicates the Dales Way and Ebor Way links onto Burley Moor. Follow the main path as its climbs steeply onto the crest of the moor. It then joins the main path along the edge of Burley Moor.

Rombald's Moor – of which Burley Moor forms a part – is a whole series of open commons where local farmers have grazing rights. Thanks to the CROW Act most open common land now enjoys full public access.

This section of the walk offers more panoramic views across Wharfedale. As you gain height, the views become increasingly impressive, with the town of Burley in the foreground, the village of Askwith across the River Wharfe and Denton Moors beyond. The route

(Above) White Wells – this eighteenth century bath house, now a celebrated viewpoint, is where Ilkley's fame as the heather spa began.
(Left) The line of the old Roman Road from Olicana to Ribchester follows its legendary straight line above Draughton.

is easy to follow, losing and regaining little height at Crag Slack and Green Crag Slack before crossing the crown of the hill to the Cow and Calf Rocks – so named because of the massive single crag (the Cow) and its smaller, freestanding boulder (the Calf). This local landmark is a popular nursery slope for climbers.

Unless you are heading towards the pub on the right, bear left behind the Cow and Calf, taking the path which heads due south-west up towards the moor, soon crossing over the stream at Backstone Beck. Then take the path half right which climbs up and over into Rocky Valley – a magnificent dry valley. Follow the path down as it joins the main path from Dick

Hudson's Inn down to White Wells.

This little eighteenth century bath-house – a notable viewpoint – is where Ilkley's history as a spa town began, invalids being carried up from boarding houses in the town to take the 'cure' – immersion into the icy waters of the spring that still flows from an ancient well behind White House. At weekends and holiday times the bath-house is open for public viewing and there are refreshment facilities available.

If you are going back to Ilkley the best route down is to the right of the platform area in front of White Wells, heading past the two Ilkley tarns, past Darwin Gardens and down Mill Gill with its pretty streamside path.

If continuing to Addingham and Skipton, take the main drive down from White Wells across the little ford and along the newly improved path to the left. This follows the hillside keeping straight ahead as it climbs to join the tarmac road towards Keighley Gate. The path continues along the moor edge, past gardens, a reservoir and then along another magnificent section of moor to the Swastika Stone – an ancient Bronze Age carved stone representing the Indo-European symbol of eternal life.

Rombald's Moor and Ilkley Moor in particular are especially rich in cup and ring stone markings. This is another magnificent viewpoint, with Beamsley Beacon and Upper Wharfedale especially notable, with Bolton Priority a distinctive feature in the foreground.

Follow the moorland path for a distance of around 1.5 miles to where, on a rise, there is a view south into Airedale, with the Doubler Stones, wind-carved crags, forming another landmark. Look for a natural gap in the crags to the right – this is Windgate Nick, again quite possibly a prehistoric track linking Wharfedale and Airedale. Take the path that slopes diagonally to the right, soon swinging north over stiles and alongside field walls to the lane at Addingham Moorside. Left here along Moorside Lane for 200 metres.

The path is now waymarked as the Millennium Way. Follow it via School Wood Farm, High House and High Brockabank, over the lane to Gildersber (the path turns left between the last buildings at the farm and then curves round in a long loop). Head by Dark Wood to the A65 Addingham by-pass. Cross carefully, keeping left as the path twists down to Marchup Beck. The path to the right over the footbridge leads into Addingham village, but otherwise cross the stepping stones and then climb to the right between allotments to the main Keighley road by a bus stop. Cross, the path continuing left through the edge of the playing field into Turner Lane. Keep left to the next main cross road at Moor Lane – a cul-de-sac – where a footpath crosses the Addingham by-pass. Cross with great care.

Continue along Moor Lane, a quiet lane that gradually climbs Addingham Low Moor, after just over half a mile becoming an unsurfaced track between fields. This is the former Roman road and was in constant use for centuries until, in 1755, the Otley-Skipton turnpike road was opened on an easier gradient past what is now Chelker Reservoir. The turnpike consigned the old road to history – and now a much-valued route for walkers, horse riders and mountain bikers. Addingham became a coaching town, where horses could be changed before climbing Chelker Brow – hence the large number of inns in the village.

After height is gained this is level, easy walking. Where the Silsden road crosses, notice the old seventeenth century guide stoop in the wall corner. Follow the old road, through gates, as it climbs around the edge of Skipton Moor and begins a gentle descent into Skipton. There are splendid views across the town of its castle, parish church and modern Building Society offices – a notable landmark.

Above the outskirts of Skipton the road becomes a steep, winding, heavily eroded path through pine trees before suddenly being transformed – at an old tollbooth – into Short Bank Road. Follow the road under the Grassington branch railway to join Otley Road and Newmarket Street in the centre of Skipton. Pubs, cafes, shops, bus and train station are straight ahead.

Between two Spas

ILKLEY TO HARROGATE

This is a cross-dale walk on a grand scale, joining two famous Yorkshire spa towns. Starting from Ilkley and the wooded banks of the River Wharfe, the route crosses the wild expanse of Denton Moor joining Badgergate, an ancient packhorseway, before descending into Washburndale. It goes through the village of Timble and along the banks of Swinsty Reservoir, before following the Harrogate Dales Way link through Haveragh Park, Harlow Carr and the Valley Gardens to the very centre of Harrogate.

FACT FILE

Distance: 19 miles (30 kilometres)

Maps: Harvey Dales East; OS Explorer 297

Terrain: Woodland and moorland paths, green tracks and farm roads. Some steady ascents and boggy stretches, but generally easy going.

Refreshment and accommodation: Sun Inn, Norwood – open daily, all day, food. Harrogate Arms, Harlow – evenings and weekend lunchtime only. Café at Harlow Car Gardens. Wide choice of inns and cafes in Harrogate. B&B accommodation in both Ilkley and Harrogate.

Toilets: Ilkley, Harrogate only.

Transport: Outward: Frequent Metrotrain services Leeds/Bradford to Ilkley, X84 bus from Leeds, Otley. Return: Frequent train and bus service 36 to Leeds, 652, 653, 904 to Otley and Bradford.

Stage point: Sun Inn (11 miles) served by service 802 on summer Sundays; or follow paths from Swinsty Hall past Fewston Reservoir to the A59 by Blubberhouses Church (11 miles) for X59 Skipton-Harrogate bus (Monday to Saturday only).

Drivers: Park Leeds and take trains or park Otley to catch frequent X84 to Ilkley; return on 652/3, 904 hourly to Otley from Harrogate.

Route

Ilkley, sheltered between the great curving bracken and heather covered fellsides of Ilkley and Denton Moors, may now be a busy West Yorkshire commuter town on the edge of the Yorkshire Dales, but is in fact one of the oldest inhabited sites of Wharfedale, being at various times a Celtic settlement, a Roman fort (Olicana) and Anglo-Viking village. In the eighteenth and nineteenth centuries it had a brief period of fame as the Malvern of the North or Heather Spa, famed for its pure air and icy cold waters, key ingredients of once fashionable hydropathic treatment that attracted such notables as Charles Darwin for the cure.

From Ilkley station forecourt turn right, then head down Brook Street to the river and along the south bank to the suspension bridge before crossing Denton Road and entering Middleton Woods. This area of exceptionally lovely deciduous woodland, noted for its splendid displays of bluebells in spring, belongs to the people of Bradford District and is open to the public. It was threatened with a major road building scheme in the 1980s by a proposed five-lane Ilkley by-pass, which would have skirted the wood's northern edge, a scheme now thankfully dormant. The path through the woods crosses Curley Hill, before eventually climbing up to the lane above the wood, bearing left to a cross roads. Turn right here.

The path follows a quiet lane to the right and

uphill. The gateway marked with a cross at the road corner was part of the former Middleton Monastery grounds, established in the nineteenth century by a notable Catholic family and in use as a religious retreat until comparatively recently. For this reason the track here was known by generations of ramblers as 'Catholic Gate' mainly because of a large religious statue that once stood here. The open views enjoyed on this and the next sections of the walk, back towards Ilkley and into Wharfedale, are exceptionally fine.

The track leads uphill past cottages and through a gate alongside the wood. The route now follows a path, right, along the field edge to a junction of tracks, before continuing up Parks Lane to open moorland, alongside a wall and fence to West Moor House Farm. The route leads through the farmyard, continuing alongside a fence towards East Moor Farm. Before the farm the path descends left alongside a wooded gill to reach a little valley and a hidden footbridge over the stream.

Fairy Dell, an attractive Pennine gill, was so named by sentimental Victorian Guidebook writers and was once part of a popular walk from Ilkley. Few walkers now come this way and you'll find the path a little overgrown.

The track continues up the far side of Fairy Dell towards Hollingley Farm. Beyond the last gate before the farm, the path returns through an adjacent field gate to the left and back to the far side of the wall, then up the left-hand side of the wall through gates to a gate onto Denton Moor.

The path bears right through heather. It is easier to follow the lower, more defined path thirty to forty metres from the wall, then bear across the moor, using a plantation of round-topped pine trees as a bearing, to cross a shallow plank bridge over a stream. The path, less distinct, joins the shooting track from Denton at Cross Bank. The route turns left up the track past shooting butts to a small shooting lodge (private property). Where it narrows, the route continues to the cairn straight ahead.

This is Lippersley Pike, at 330 metres the highest point on the walk, a magnificent viewpoint and welcome windbreak. There are views across the whole moorland area, into the

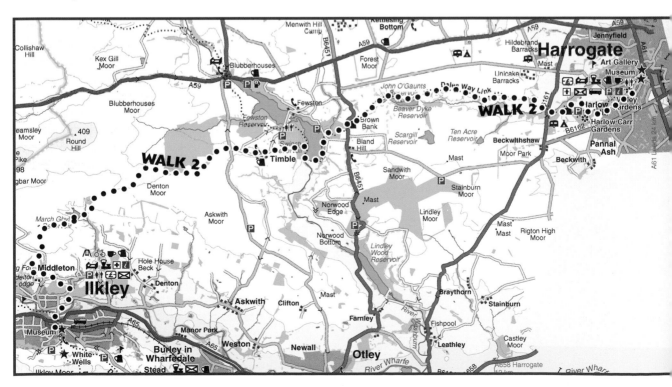

Wharfe and Washburn valleys, and Leeds beyond. This is an area rich in historic remains – cairns, barrows and cup and ring marked rocks – as well as ancient tracks and a stretch of almost invisible Roman Road from Olicana (Ilkley) to Alborough. Particularly interesting is the narrow stony path which is now followed – this is High Badger gate, an ancient peddlers' path between Skipton, Addingham and Knaresborough (Badger is the old word for peddler; hence "to badger" someone). A more modern and somewhat more sinister landmark is the "Golf Balls" – the USA electronic surveillance station at Menwith Hill to the north-east.

The route now follows High Badgergate above Cop Hirst and to Ellarcar Pike, another viewpoint, to join a stony lane. This meets the farm track to the Blubberhouses road, continuing along the lane ahead, forking right to

Fairy Dell – a forgotten gill, once popular with Victorian guidebook writers.

Timble.

It is remarkable that the intimate little village of Timble so close to the great conurbations of Leeds and Bradford has remained so unspoiled, no doubt because of restrictions on building by respective water boards safeguarding their water catchment grounds. It is now enjoying a more welcoming kind of protection as part of the Nidderdale Area of Outstanding Natural Beauty. As well as attractive cottage gardens there is an old roadside well and the Robinson Institute – the village hall built in 1884 thanks to the generosity of an American benefactor whose family came from Timble. The former Timble Inn was for generations a popular hostelry frequented by walkers and cyclists from Leeds but has recently closed.

The lane behind Timble forks left to a narrow, enclosed green way through gates and across open fields down to Swinsty Moor Plantation, and a pleasant path through the woods, alongside the wall of Swinsty Hall gardens. Built in 1570, but much extended in later years, Swinsty Hall is a magnificent Elizabethan and Jacobean yeoman's house, with many fine architectural features.

The route now follows the stony track around Swinsty Reservoir and across the dam. From the dam end turn left along the drive, and soon after a small bridge over the stream takes the path left through woods by the water's edge.

Swintsy Reservoir is one of the great chain of reservoirs along the River Washburn built by Leeds Corporation in 1876 to supply the city with fresh drinking water. Covering 63 hectares, this is a popular place for birdwatching, with a wide variety of native and migrant species, especially in the winter months.

The second part of this walk follows the Harrogate-Bolton Abbey Dales Way link. It is clearly signed throughout with green and yellow Dales Way waymarks and yellow arrows. From the lane the route follows the reservoir arm, before turning sharp right through woods, eventually to reach the main road at Bramelane. The Sun Inn is a few metres to the left (refreshments).

From the Sun Inn the Dales Way leads behind the car park, across a shallow valley over stiles below Bank End Farm, into an enclosed green way. This steep and ancient embankment known as Bank Slack was part of the boundary of Haveragh Park, a medieval deer park. According to legend it was given to Adam Haveragh by John of Gaunt as a result of a wager when Adam, a cripple, hobbled eight miles in a single day around the perimeter of the park. It is an important water gathering ground and for many years all public access was denied by the local Water Board until a famous court case in the 1960s. A ramblers' champion, Corrie Gaunt of Harrogate, then won a landmark court case to prove that such rights existed. This has enabled this path to be enjoyed by many thousands of walkers ever since.

The path, waymarked, leads through gates and over stiles. At the crossroads take the path right signed to Pot Bridge and Dales Way, along the hillside above John o' Gaunt's Reservoir. There is a fine viewpoint over the upper reservoir from here. The track continues alongside and above the reservoirs, through gates, to a junction with a metalled farm track at Long Liberty Farm. The route turns left here, through gates to the farm, beyond which it turns sharp right (waymarked) through more farm gates.

The track now follows walls and the top side of fields above a shallow valley to join a track to Central House Farm, then along a metalled lane past Prospect House Farm. Where the drive turns sharp right, the route keeps ahead past Whin Hill Farm, through gates and stiles, alongside a long stone wall above pastures. About 800 metres before The Oatlands, the path bends sharp right around a small plantation to reach the farm, and along the farm drive to Pot Bridge Farm and the junction with the B6161.

This must be crossed with care – fast

Lippersley Pike – ancient cairn and viewpoint on the medieval Badgergate packhorseway across Denton Moor.

heavy traffic – before descending to Pot Bridge, a lovely medieval bridge. The path on the left cuts the corner up to the cottage. A right-of-way passes in front of the cottage (there is an unofficial diversion around the garden 60 metres above) into Cardale Woods. At a junction the route keeps along the higher path above the valley, before losing height and bearing right, behind Harlow Carr Gardens, then straight ahead at a junction, before finally bearing left to the Harrogate Arms. The path reaches a lane and turns right for 100 metres where, opposite the entrance to Harlow Carr Gardens, a metal barrier indicates the path into Oakdale Woods.

Harlow Carr, formerly under the auspices of the Northern Horticultural Society, is one of the showpieces of ornamental gardens and plant life in the north of England – there is also a restaurant and shop.

The path goes alongside Oakdale Woods, then crosses a busy road to enter Valley Gardens. A delightful walk passes many of the original springs or wells that made Harrogate famous and leads into the centre of the town. Bus and rail stations, cafes and inns are straight ahead.

Sharp Haw and Elbolton

SKIPTON TO GRASSINGTON

From Craven's principle market to the capital of Upper Wharfedale, this walk takes in one of the most spectacular viewpoints in the southern Dales. Paths along Flasby and Hetton Beck join the old green road to Cracoe. From here the route follows the quiet lane past Threaplands, from where a

little moorland pass leads over the shoulder of Elbolton, one of the seven remarkable reef knolls of Craven, then through the hamlet of Thorpe along field paths to Grassington.

Route

From Skipton bus or rail station head to the High Street, dominated on four days a week by a colourful market, and continue beyond the castle and parish church over Mill Bridge onto the Grassington Road, before bearing right along a cul-de-sac road, Chapel Hill. Keep left at the fork, and where the lane ends go through a stile onto a path, which climbs steeply up behind the town and castle, to a stile in the wall above. It was here in the Civil War that Cromwell positioned a battery of cannon to blast the castle walls, but the castle never surrendered.

Continue along the path as it descends to reach and cross the main A65 road. Cross with care to avoid very high-speed traffic. A stile ahead leads into the golf course. Follow the waymarked route through the Old Park, eventually leaving the golf course to join and turn left into Brackenley Lane.

Although only a minor road, this is a frequently used by drivers as a short cut, so continue to take care for the 400 metres or so across Tarn Moor to the junction with the busy and dangerous B6265. Keep straight ahead on the field path opposite that leads to the lane from Stirton. Follow this lane as it zigzags round two sharp corners. The route now follows a bridlepath towards Sharp Haw ahead. Leave the main track after 300 metres, the bridlepath being a slightly muddy route, marked

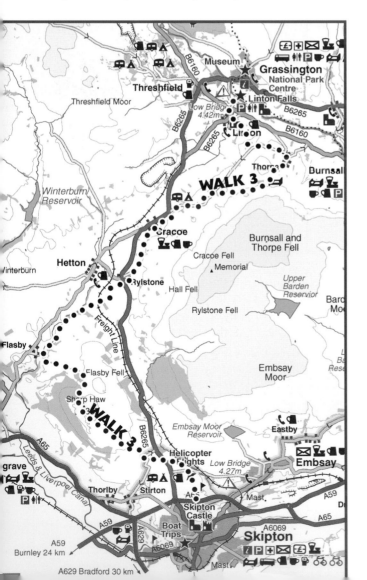

Winter snow covers Butterhaw, one of the smallest of the seven reef knolls of Craven.

by stakes, which climbs steeply up open moorland. Head directly for the summit of Sharp Haw (some 200 metres to the west of the official bridleway, but this is now Access Land).

At 357 metres Sharp Haw may not be especially high but commands extensive views across the Aire Gap to Pendle Hill and the Bowland hills beyond. To the east is Embsay Crag and Barden Moor, and below the rolling drumlins, created from glacial waste left behind after the last Ice Age.

The descent from the summit follows the wall to the right, over the stile and along a path that eventually joins the main path between Sharp Haw and its near neighbour Rough Haw. Turn left down the path which soon becomes a clear track, through gates towards Flasby.

Cross the stream at the bridge just before the village. A gate on the right gives access to

FACT FILE

Distance: 12.5 miles (20 kilometres).

Maps: Harvey Dales South; OS Explorer OL2.

Terrain: Mainly field paths and moorland tracks, but some sections of quiet lane. One steep ascent to the summit of Sharp Haw.

Refreshment and accommodation: Angel Inn, Hetton. Devonshire Arms, Cracoe. Café in Cracoe village. Choice of pubs, cafes and B&B in Grassington.

Toilets: Skipton, Linton Falls, Grassington

Transport: Outward: Regular trains Leeds-Skipton; Bus X84 from Leeds, Otley, Ilkley. Return: Hourly buses 72/67A to Skipton (daily), two hourly to Ilkley (74 - weekdays) occasional Dalesbuses on Sundays and Bank Holidays to Ilkley or Leeds.

Stage point: Cracoe (12km 7.5 miles) with hourly buses (67A/72) to Skipton.

Drivers: Park Skipton and walk – return on the 67A/72 bus from Grassington.

a section of bridlepath, which follows the stream, crossing a track and barn at Holme Laithe, keeping along the hillside above Flasby Beck and going through a series of fields, the route marked by stiles or gates. This continues for about a mile (1.3km) before descending to a footbridge over the stream. If heading for Hetton and the Angel, the route is straight ahead, otherwise cross the stream and head up to the right past Mill Gate Lathe to a bridge over the freight-only Swinden Quarry branch railway line. Keep ahead to reach an enclosed path that curves by tall beech hedges into the village of Rylstone.

Go past the pond to the main road and cross to the lane to Rylstone Church, beyond which is a path past the farm and the long vanished ruins of Rylstone Hall. This was the home of the ill-fated Norton family who perished in the abortive Rising of the North in 1569 when local Catholic families supported a rebellion against Queen Elizabeth I. The stone tower on the hillside south of Rylstone was the summer house of the Nortons, whose members faced

Thorpe Green – a quiet corner of Wharfedale's 'hidden village'

execution and loss of their lands, a history recalled in Wordsworth's elegiac poem the White Doe of Rylstone.

Take the lane past the sunken hollows of the fishponds to follow the pre-turnpike road known as Chapel Lane to Cracoe, with its welcoming inn and café.

From Cracoe follow the main road (with a pavement on the far side) for 400 metres to where it bends and Thorpe Lane bears off to the right. This quiet and picturesque lane climbs for almost a mile (1.2km) past Threapland and Skelterton and later Butter Haw Hill, two of the celebrated reef knolls of Craven. These are hills of almost pure limestone, distilled like coral reefs out of the bodies of ancient sea-creatures when this part of the Dales was part of a shallow, tropical sea in Carboniferous times some 250 million years ago. There are now only six of the reef knolls, as one, Swinden, across the valley, has been quarried for the purity of its limestone and is now a gigantic cavity.

Look for the footpath, right, by a gate and stile, with a sign to Thorpe. The path crosses rough pastureland, marked by stiles, before gradually ascending the shoulder of the next hill, Elbolton. It joins a grassy track between Elbolton and Stebden to the south, which forms a natural pass between the two knolls.

Elbolton is sometimes referred to in older, more sentimental guidebooks as the 'Hill of Fairies', perhaps ancient folk memory of the Bronze and Iron Age peoples who lived in settlements and caves in and around the hill, a source of many important archaeological finds. As this is now Access Land you can take one of the many paths to the summit, a fine viewpoint looking across to Grassington and Grass Wood.

Continue along the track, which now descends steeply into Thorpe. This is the so-called 'hidden village', which according to legend was missed by marauding Scots during their many violent forages into Wharfedale in the fourteenth century. In later years it was reputed to be a centre for shoemakers and cobblers, but little evidence remains. It is, however, perhaps one of the least changed and unspoiled villages in the Yorkshire Dales, having had scarcely any new development over the past century.

Pass the little enclosed green to head left at the junction, then bear left again, once more entering Thorpe Lane. It is here a narrow lane, curving around the north slopes of Elbolton, with fine views across the dale towards Grassington and Hebden. After around 400 metres a bridle gate leads to a narrow, enclosed path, scarcely wide enough for a human let alone a horse. Follow it as its zigzags downhill, eventually crossing a couple of fields to reach the main Burnsall road. Cross to a stile slightly to your right, which leads to another path bearing left and marked by stiles. This

Patterns of eighteenth century enclosure walls give special character to this Wharfedale landscape.

crosses Stickhaw Hill above Linton's Norman church and heads down to the old mill cottages at Linton Falls.

Pass the row of cottages and new housing development at the site of the old water-powered Linton Mill to locate the path on the right to Linton Falls, spectacular waterfalls where the Craven Fault crosses the River Wharfe. Go straight ahead across the bridge and up narrow Sedber Lane, better known locally as the Snake Walk, to the car park, National Park Centre and Transport Interchange for return buses. But most walkers will want to explore this delightful little former lead-mining town with a museum, interesting shops and ample opportunity for refreshment.

WALK 4

Grimwith & Stump Cross

GRASSINGTON TO PATELEY BRIDGE

FACT FILE

Distance: 14 miles (22 kilometres).

Maps: Harvey Dales South, Dales East; OS Explorer OL2, 298.

Terrain: A real mixture – upland tracks some lakeside and riverside paths, a short stretch of unavoidable busy road, as well as a certain amount of rough grazing land and open country making this tough going in places, compensated by magnificent views throughout. Some moderate ascents.

Refreshment and accommodation: Stump Cross Caverns – teas and light meals. Open daily in the summer months, weekends only in winter. Choice of cafes, pubs and B&Bs in Pateley Bridge.

Toilets: Grassington, Pateley Bridge.

Transport: Outward: Weekdays: Dales Bus 72 service from Skipton or 74 from Ilkley to Grassington. Sundays, Bank Holidays: Dales Bus 800/805 direct from Leeds and Ilkley. Return: Daily: Service 24 hourly from Pateley Bridge to Harrogate then frequent buses and trains for Leeds. Summer Sundays: Dales Bus 802 to Otley and Leeds, 24 to Harrogate.

Stage point: Summer Sundays only: Stump Cross (8 miles) by catching service 812 back to Grassington or forward to Pateley, or 802 to Otley from Greenhow cross roads (10 miles).

Drivers: Weekdays: Park Harrogate, catch X59 service to Skipton for service 72 to Grassington, then return on 24 from Harrogate. Summer Sundays: Park Pateley and catch mid-morning 812 to return to Grassington to start of walk.

This fine dale-to-dale walk linking Wharfedale and Nidderdale has only been possible since summer 2005 and the opening up of new link routes over Public Access land within the Yorkshire Dales National Park and Nidderdale AONB. The route also follows the northern shores of Grimwith Reservoir, a giant man-made lake in a spectacular upland setting.

This is also a walk with a strong lead mine theme, linking the former mine workings in Hebden Gill with the pock-marked moors above Stump Cross and Ashfield Gill in Nidderdale. Please ensure you keep to obvious paths and tracks through these areas and do not attempt to walk on or over old mine workings where there may be deep and dangerous hidden shafts.

Route

From Grassington National Park Centre and Travel Interchange proceed to the Village Square and up the Main Street to the Town Hall, turning right past the entrance and cottages then along the evocatively named Horse Gap Yett, before turning sharp left up High Lane. After 200 metres, passing a long field on the left, you reach a narrow field on the left with a gate. This is the start of the path up to Edge Lane, generally visible on the ground as it ascends diagonally across narrow fields, marked by stiles with little gates. Turn right and walk along the walled Edge Lane, savouring impressive views back towards Grassington and Linton, forward into mid-Wharfedale and

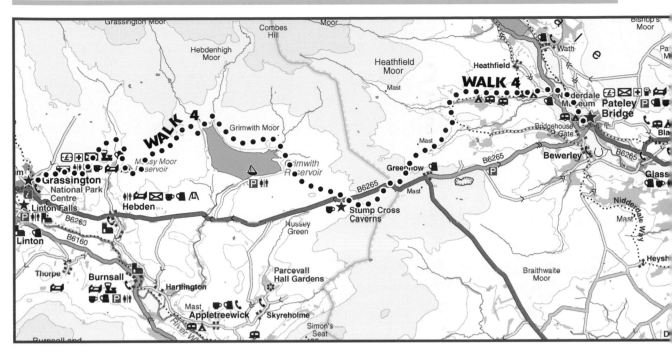

across to the heather-covered summits of Barden Moor.

Follow the main track as it curves to the right, ascending a low knoll before passing High Garnshaw Farm, becoming Tinkers' Lane as it crosses high open pastures before finally descending into Hebden Gill, an area still marked by lead mine workings including old ore crushing and washing floors.

Cross the beck at stepping stones ahead and follow the clear path leading into the narrow gully straight ahead, soon bearing right along another clear path. This climbs diagonally up the hillside, crossing through the pastures about half way up the fields, the route marked by field gates. The path climbs slowly up the edge of the moorland, again with good views into the Gill.

Soon a low dam of a small moorland reservoir, Mossy Moor, comes into view. At the next wall and stile do not cross but follow the wall past the reservoir, again with extensive open views. If you keep the wall that encloses the moor and reservoir on your right (this is now Public Access land), you will eventually find a stone stile in the wall corner which links with Backstone Edge Lane – a green lane and pub-lic bridleway. If the access area should be closed for any reason this lane can be reached via the B6265 road.

Turn left into Backstone Edge Lane, a lovely enclosed green way over Hebden Moor, through gates. The lane eventually peters out into rushes. Follow the line of the bridlepath (there is a narrow path to the right of the very overgrown way) alongside the wall and through gates as it turn northwards. Where the wall becomes a wire fence near Knotts Top, head across open moorland (still a bridleway) and towards the rickety gate about 100 metres above the wall corner. The path now follows a ruined wall on the left.

Knotts Well below you is also Public Access land, but an unpleasant, wet, rush-infested bog, so head for the far wall and fence. Turn right, down the edge of the field to where a rickety gate or a new stile delivers you to a few metres below the busy footpath around Grimwith Reservoir.

Grimwith is Yorkshire Water's largest reservoir, opened in 1983 when an existing Victorian reservoir was dramatically increased in size. It now covers 147 hectares and when full contains around 4,790 million gallons of water.

The track swings eastwards over the foot-bridge at Bracken Haw and becomes a pleasant path along the northern rim of the reservoir, with fine lakeside views, usually animated by the coloured sails of yachts or windsurfers. Follow the way as it curves to the right over the little headland past the former Grimwith House farm, 200 metres beyond which a stile on the left indicates the path to Stump Cross. Before taking this path you may wish to take a look at the carefully restored monastic barn on the headland some 100 metres ahead. This little laithe or barn was formerly part of a grange of Bolton Abbey at Grimwith and was carefully re-erected, complete with authentic ling thatching, when the reservoir was extended.

The path to Stump Cross climbs past High

Ling thatched barn, Grimwith. This unique monastic field barn was carefully rebuilt in the 1980s with authentic ling thatch, once the most common roofing material for cottages and barns in the Dales.

Shaw Laithe over rough pasture and moorland, bearing right over stiles at the craggy outcrop of Knot Head before descending to the main road. Cross, and a few metres to the right is a gate leading into rough pasture. However you may well wish to walk the 250 metres along the grassy verge up the main road to enjoy refreshments (toilets available for patrons) at Stump Cross Caverns.

Stump Cross takes its name from the long-vanished remains of an ancient monastic cross on the old drovers' road between Malham and Grassington via Pateley Bridge, which became a turnpike road to serve the lead mines in the early nineteenth century. The remarkable show caves, discovered by lead miners, are rich in geological and archaeological interest and well worth a visit.

Return to the gate into the rough pasture below to continue the walk. This is an area of Public Access land, which walkers have a legal right to cross. Do so with caution, and follow all way marks and warning signs. Avoid all obvious old mine workings, hollows or slopes, which may cover dangerous shafts. Cross the pasture that descends into a shallow valley known as Dry Gill. Turn left to locate a stile in the crossing wall and keep straight ahead along the wallside in the narrow, dry valley below Stump Cross before joining the line of a clear green track bearing up to the left. The track heads to an old (fenced off) mine building. Keep to the right of this building along a narrow path which soon joins a clear track, and eventually the public right of way over Sun Side Allotments – look for waymarks – before emerging on the busy B6265 at a gate just west of Keld Houses.

The next 400 metres of the walk is less than satisfactory. Turn right along the main road, which has narrow grassy verges as it curves around twin bends. Keep on the verge in single file and cross carefully where necessary before reaching a footpath on the far side of an isolated house, just as you pass the Greenhow sign. The path leads to an enclosed way above Gill Beck and past Far Side farm (follow the waymarks). It becomes part of the Nidderdale

Industrial Heritage Trail – again follow the way-marks, past interpretive panels, to the lead mining area of Brandstone Beck, joining the main track through recently disturbed mine tailings.

Go left over the bridge across the beck, climbing out of the valley along the track towards Near Hardcastle. Waymarks indicate the sharp right turn on the track above Near Hardcastle before joining the Nidderdale Way as it curves around the hillside known as Nabs. Turn left along the Way, descending to some quite spectacular mine workings and tips above the Ashfold valley. At a junction of paths, take the narrower way which skirts to the left and below the main tips, curving round and to the right above Ashfold Beck. It crosses an impressive man-made scree slope before descending to a footbridge over the beck.

Ascend to the main path, and follow the

Ashfield Side – in parts of Upper Nidderdale intensive lead mines and ore working have created an almost lunar landscape

track, through gates, down the Ashfold Valley soon reaching tarmac and two large caravan sites, along what is now Foster Beck. Keep right at the junction with the lane to join the main road to Ramsgill by Cove Close, taking the signed footpath to the right of the farm that leads towards the river. Keep right at the little footbridge over Foster Beck by Brigg House to join the path along the Nidd, a lovely riverside way along the floodbank that eventually emerges in Pateley at the little park by the bridge. Cross the bridge to the cafes, pubs and shops of the town centre, with the bus station for Harrogate or Otley on your immediate left.

WALK 5
The Washburn Way
OTLEY TO PATELEY BRIDGE

The little River Washburn, a tributary of the Wharfe, provides the city of Leeds with much of its water supply, feeding a chain of spectacular reservoirs that have created what is sometimes called 'Yorkshire's Little Lake District'. The walk follows the Washburn almost to its source, along a now neglected route once popular in the pre-car age when hikers walked in their thousands into Washburndale from train stations or bus stops at Otley, Pool or even the busy Leeds tram terminus at White Cross, Guiseley. After linking the three popular circular trails around Swinsty, Fewston and Thruscross Reservoirs, lanes and paths connect to a fine route into Nidderdale to terminate the walk in Pateley Bridge.

FACT FILE

Distance: 22,5 miles (36 kilometres).

Maps: Harvey Dales East; OS Explorer 26, 27.

Terrain: Mostly riverside or lakeside paths and tracks, but some short sections of road walking and field paths. Gradients mostly gradual and gentle.

Refreshment and accommodation: Hopper Lane, Inn, Blubberhouses (over half a mile – 900 metres along A59). Choice of cafés pubs, B&B in Pateley Bridge.

Toilets: Otley, Fewston Dam (in Yorkshire Water car park), Pateley Bridge.

Transport: Outward: Frequent bus services X84 Leeds-Otley-Ilkley. 967 bus from Menston Station. 653/904 bus hourly from Harrogate. Return: Hourly buses 24 to Harrogate, 802 (summer Sundays) from Pateley Bridge and Blubberhouses to Otley and Leeds.

Stage point: Blubberhouses (12.5 miles – 20 kilometres) with bus service every two/three hours (weekdays only) to Harrogate or Skipton. Bus stops on A59 opposite Blubberhouses church. On Sundays take or catch the 802 either at the Sun Inn, Norwood, or at the end of the lane from Blubberhouses to Greenhow.

Drivers: Weekdays: Park Otley, return on 24 or X59 to Harrogate, then 653 or 904 to Otley. Summer Sundays: Park Otley and return on 802.

Route

From Otley bus station head to the bridge and riverside gardens. Follow the riverside path, past flower beds, the weir and play areas. Where the park ends at the concrete bridge, keep directly ahead along the old riverside byway – in effect a footpath, overgrown with balsam and nettles in late summer. Follow the river, with Farnley Park to your left, across large arable fields, for 1.5 miles (2km) to where, as the river bears slightly right, a faint green track crosses a concrete base. Look for where a length of fence appears in the long hedge to the left, and where a bridlegate leads into the lane from Farnley.

Turn right, on going over Leathley Bridge and past the lodge into the main Leathley road. Cross with care – this is a dangerous road with fast moving traffic – to walk along the narrow verge into Leathley village, past the church, eventually crossing to a slightly broader pavement on the right. At the end of the village by Leathley Mill (now a private house) a narrow path left, signed Norwood Edge, leads between a high wooden fence and wall, behind the old mill buildings. The path, waymarked, leads to the banks of the River

Washburn before bearing right at a stile up the old (now dry) mill leat embankment. Follow this, soon passing the trout farm, to emerge on a lane. Cross and go slightly right to pick up a lovely woodland path above the river which soon passes the dam and follows the shores of Lindley Wood Reservoir, with attractive views of the water between trees.

At the B6451 turn left over the viaduct, then right, over the stile and first right along the usually dry headwaters of the reservoir, eventually reaching a gate leading over the bridge to rejoin the banks of the River Washburn. Keep along the river so reaching Dob Park Bridge, a fine old packhorse bridge by a ford on a once important routeway between Otley and Knaresborough or Ripon. Given there is now (usually) so little water in the River Washburn, most of it being used to feed the households of Leeds, it is difficult to imagine a time when the bridge provided a safe, dry crossing for people and horses over a rushing moorland river.

Cross the bridge, the path now meandering alongside then away from the river, marked by stiles, bearing right through the wood and across Snowden Beck, before returning to the Washburn. Where Timble Gill Beck meets the river down a little side valley there is a tiny hump-backed bridge, built in the late 1960s by the West Riding Ramblers' Association to commemorate the life and work of their former honorary secretary and lifelong campaigner for rights of access, Alderman Arthur Adamson. Cross the bridge and then take the steppingstones to the left over the main river – if the river is in spate there is a bridge some 400 metres upstream. Follow the path along the far side of the river, eventually as the grassy embankment of Swinsty Dam comes into view, bearing right to follow the rim of the valley up to the dam.

Do not cross, but keep ahead along the main drive towards Fewston, crossing a bridge and taking the permissive path, left, along the shores of Swinsty Reservoir. Yorkshire Water have provided generous public access to their

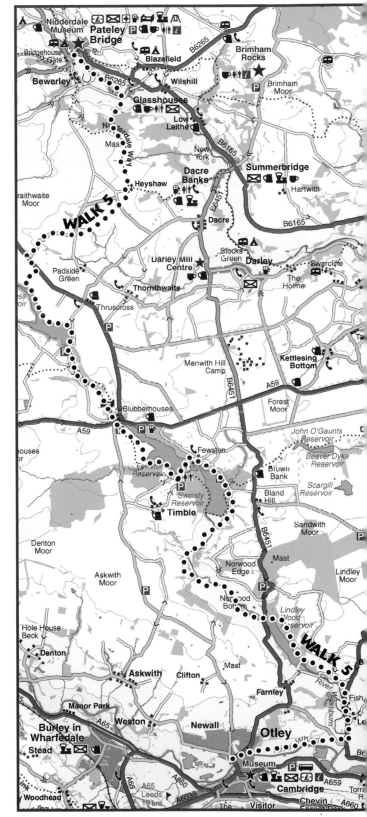

The fine riverside park at Otley is both a focal point for the town and an appropriate starting point for a walk into Washburndale.

catchment lands, with excellent permissive footpath routes close to all their main reservoirs, but it is vital to keep away from the water's edge and all reservoir buildings and structures at all times.

This path eventually joins the lane that crosses a small viaduct over the easterly arm of the reservoir by the main car park (Route 2 for Harrogate crosses this point). Return to the reservoir side, following the attractive shoreline, usually busy with walkers, to emerge at Fewston Dam. Cross the dam, but take the first gate on the right to join the path that continues along the western bank of Fewston Reservoir (toilets are a further 100 metres ahead along the road in the main car park). This is a particularly lovely high-level path with fine open views, curving around the long western arm of the reservoir where Thackray Beck comes in, eventually to emerge on the A59 at

the Blubberhouses car park. Turn right. The Hopper Lane Inn is ten minutes walk away along a busy road, if you are waiting for more than a few minutes for the X59 bus.

Otherwise cross the A59 with extreme care beyond the crash barriers (average speed of traffic is around 80mph) and turn left to go down the ladder stile just beyond the river bridge. This leads to another permissive Yorkshire Water riverside path along the river, through the woods, past a cricket ground and old mill race and pond, eventually crossing the river at a footbridge. Keep along the river to emerge at the old construction area below Thruscross Dam. If you are lucky there will be a shimmering column of water down the 39 metre (129 feet) high dam. Completed in 1966, construction of the fourth and newest of the Washburn reservoirs required the total removal and rebuilding of the now flooded hamlet of West End.

Steps on the left lead from the valley floor to the dam top, just below the car park. Turn right over the dam, following the lane for half a mile (800 metres) gently uphill, to where, on the left, a stile leads to a path. This joins a track down to the reservoir edge and a path with fine, open views along the embankment. The artificial lake, covering 58 hectares and containing 7,842 cubic metres or 1,725 million gallons of water, enjoys a remote but beautiful setting, and is at its best after spring or autumn rains when well filled and otherwise muddy reservoir shorelines are covered. As the path crosses into woodland and bears right to climb onto open heather moorland, there are spectacular views as far as Barden Fell and its crags above Wharfedale.

Follow the path over a large step stile, about 120 metres beyond which, opposite a low outcropping crag and by a post, you must turn right at ninety degrees. Head for the wall 200 metres to the right, over what is now Public Access land to where, in the wall, you will see a field gate. This accesses the main

Greenhow road, Duck Street, a racetrack of a road. Cross with care to the broad verge opposite, and turn left for 400 metres to meet the junction with Braithwaite Lane.

Follow this quiet lane for around a mile (1.6km) to its junction with the Padside lane. There are parallel footpaths but these are partially blocked and difficult to follow – careful pathfinding is needed in this section. Keep ahead on the farm track, a bridleway, to Banger House Farm, just beyond which a path heads north-eastwards alongside a wall and

This tiny footbridge over Timble Beck was erected in 1967 by members of the West Riding Ramblers Association. It is in memory of their former secretary Alderman Arthur Adamson, Leeds City Councillor and lifelong campaigner for footpaths and public access.

across a field to Grange House, from where the path goes along the farm drive to Dyke Lane ahead. Cross the lane, stiles and a sign marking the path to Heyshaw, keeping right to head between buildings via gates to the centre of the hamlet. Turn right to the cross-roads, then left with the Nidderdale Way signs, along a track to Hill Top farm. Take the path alongside open moorland towards the radio mast ahead, a magnificent viewpoint looking down into Nidderdale from the summit of Guise Cliff.

Go right, just before the radio mast, over a stile, on a path which slopes into Guise Cliff Wood, soon bearing left into the wood. At a fork keep left, eventually to head down towards a beautiful small lake, Guisecliff Tarn, hidden within the wood. From the boulders at

(Left) The Washburn valley above Blubberhouses – one of several permissive paths provided by Yorkshire Water for public enjoyment of their land.
(Right) Looking over to Barden Fell from the top of Thruscross Reservoir and Washburndale.

the end of the lake, bear right down the narrow path through Parker Wood, past Hollin Farm and Glasshouses Bridge. You can catch the 24 bus in Glasshouses if you are short of time, but a pity to miss the last mile, past mill pond and riverside, to emerge at the bridge by the old railway station (now the car park) in Pateley Bridge, with its welcoming pubs, cafes, shops and bus station.

The Fountains Walk

PATELEY BRIDGE TO RIPON

This ramble across the gentle, eastern foothills of the eastern Dales and Nidderdale AONB links two fine North Yorkshire towns and also two famous National Trust properties – Brimham Rocks and the World Heritage Site of Fountains Abbey. Throughout the walk there are extensive views, not just of Nidderdale, but across the Vale of York to the North York Moors.

Route

From Pateley Bridge bus station walk up the High Street, bearing right with the main road towards Ripon, but about 50 metres beyond the Methodist church look for an opening with stone steps on the left, signed Panorama Walk. This climbs past a Victorian stone fountain to the town cemetery. Immediately beyond, an enclosed path follows the cemetery wall to the ruined church of St Mary's. The little medieval church with its archaic cottage windows was too small and inconveniently sited for the growing town of Pateley Bridge in the early nineteenth century and in 1826 it was abandoned for the new church of St Cuthbert's nearer the town centre. It has gradually decayed into the ruin it is today, a quiet and evocative corner above the town.

The path continues through a narrow gate that leaves the churchyard just above the church and crosses fields to a narrow lane. Turn left here, along the top of Ripley Bank, enjoying good views across the dale. Keep ahead with the Nidderdale Way signs onto a green way as the lane bears right to the main B6265. Left here, taking care with traffic, for 250 metres to the cottages at Blazefield, where the lane below the cottages leads to a bridleway, still the Nidderdale Way. Keep in the same direction along tracks and a section of lane, following the Nidderdale Way signs, along a green way to another lane. Turn down and

FACT FILE

Distance: 13 miles (21 kilometres)

Maps: Harvey Dales East; OS Explorer 298.

Terrain: Tracks, field paths and green ways – some short ascents otherwise fairly easy terrain, though path finding needs time and care in the second part of the walk

Refreshment and accommodation: Sawley Arms, Sawley (limited opening times); small refreshment points at Brimham Rocks; National Trust café and restaurant at Fountains Abbey (outside pay boundary); choice of pubs and cafes in Ripon. Accommodation in Pateley Bridge and Ripon.

Toilets: Pateley Bridge, Brimham Rocks, Fountains Abbey, Ripon.

Transport: Outward: Harrogate & District service 24 (hourly) on weekdays, less frequent Sundays; summer Sundays Dales Bus 802 from Leeds and Otley to Pateley and Fountains Abbey, 812 from York. Return: Frequent Harrogate & District bus services 36 from Ripon to Harrogate and Leeds; summer Sundays 802 to Leeds via Otley, 812 to York.

Stage point: Two miles walk from Brimham Rocks (4 miles) by path or lane to Summerbridge for service 24; or from Fountains Abbey Visitor Centre (10 miles) 802, 812 on summer Sundays only. There is also a limited weekday Ripon Rowler minibus service, but the last return is early afternoon.

Drivers: Park Harrogate and take 24 bus to Pateley Bridge, returning on (frequent) 36 to Harrogate.

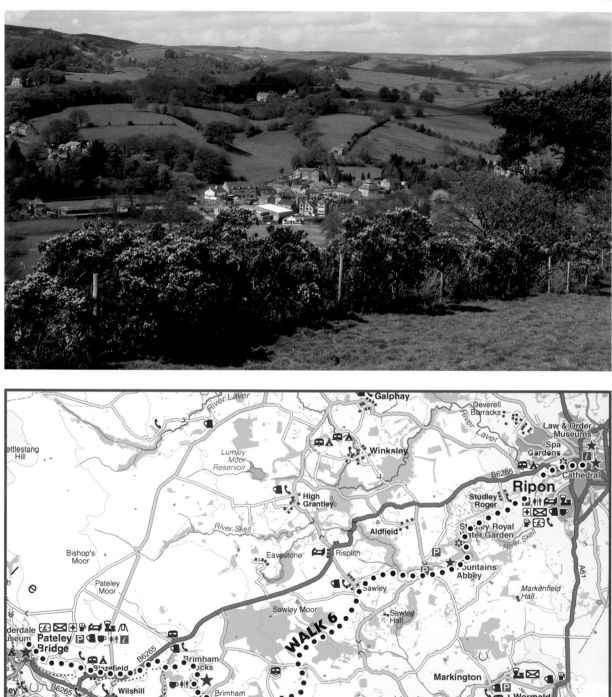

(Opposite) Looking across to the village of Bewerley from above St Mary's Church, Pateley Bridge.
(This page, left) Brimham Rocks – the wind carved rocks of Brimham are always popular with visitors.
(Right) Lacan Cross – a boundary cross on the former Fountains estate.

around a double bend to a track, left, which follows the edge of open heath, above farm buildings, to emerge at White House farm.

Keep ahead on the Nidderdale Way to the next farm where a path, this time signed to Brimham Rocks, descends to the right and curves to the left to reach Fellback (way-marked) and cross the stream at a footbridge. Follow the obvious track uphill, maintaining the same direction alongside woods, with a field wall to your left (ignore stiles into the wood). Continue along North Pasture, eventually climbing to a stile before bearing and curving left towards the farm. The path passes just above the farm. Follow the farm track as it

climbs away from the farm, but at a bend a stile on the right leads into Brimham Rocks. Follow the path as it winds through bilberry and trees, edging between boulders, before climbing steeply to the great plateau with its massive, wind-carved, sandstone crags.

This 50-acre National Trust property contains an extraordinary collection of huge natural sandstone formations, carved into exotic shapes, which were given fanciful names by the Victorians such as the Dancing Bear, Druid's Altar and The Pulpit. It is a lovely area to wander around, with glorious views along and down Nidderdale.

Make your way between the rocks, past the Visitor Centre, heading along the main path and drive towards the main entrance. Turn right along the road for 60 metres to where the Nidderdale Way is again rejoined, now a beautiful path crossing the open expanse of Brimham Moor, with heather and birch trees. Keep ahead past Riva Hill where a track is joined, meeting the drive from Riva Farm. At the junction of ways, there are, on a clear day, magnificent views across the towns

Fountains Abbey – a World Heritage Site.

of Harrogate and Knaresborough to the lower Aire Valley power stations with even a distant glimpse of York Minister. Turn left here, leaving the Nidderdale Way to descend to the stream and wood west of Beckside Farm, where a lane is reached. Follow the lane as it becomes a farm track up to Low Farm.

Care is needed here – to the immediate left and east of the farm, go through gates into what appear to be cattle pens, beyond which the final gate opens into a green track that is the bridle path to Rabbit Hill Farm (an occasional blue waymark is to be seen). Pass through two more gates but leave the main track to keep alongside the wall to another gate, where to the right of a modern house the path leads into the lane. Turn left for 300

metres to where a stile and signpost on the right indicate the path alongside the field towards the edge of the plantation ahead. Keep ahead towards Warsill Hall Farm, but just before the farm go through the wide cattle gate, left, to locate a stone stile ahead.

Cross the field to a gate in the far corner and then right alongside the wall down to a stile into the woodland below, where a steep path drops to cross the medieval Butterton Bridge, built by the monks of Fountains Abbey in the thirteenth century. Wooden steps opposite climb to a stile into the corner of a field – cross to the plantation ahead to a gate and stile into Green Lane. Almost immediately a stile leads to a path across pasture and past the Lacon Cross, a boundary cross probably indicating the ancient line of path between what was a monastic grange at Warsill and the parent abbey at Fountains.

The stile in the field corner leads to a path, which crosses a stream to another stile just before the farm at Lacon Hall. Go to the left along the farm drive but at the first gate as the track bends right, the path heads across the field to the corner where a stile takes it alongside the hedge ahead to a stone stile just south of Sawley village.

Take Low Gate Lane, left, for just over half a mile to where, as it enters woodland and bears right, a stile, left, leads into Skell Bank Wood. Descend to cross the little River Skell at the footbridge, following the track that eventually joins the lane 200 metres above the Fountains Hall entrance into the Studley Royal estate.

If you are planning to visit this magnificent World Heritage Site, with its Jacobean Fountains Hall, great medieval Cistercian abbey founded in 1132, unique monastic mill and exquisitely beautiful water gardens with their statues and temples, walk straight ahead to the pay barrier on your left. There is a choice of ways, the best being the path to the south side of the grounds, with its splendid views across to the abbey, canal and lakes. There is a café and toilets either at the main Visitor Centre above and to the left of Fountains Hall, or at the far entrance into Studley Royal estate. Pass the lake into the deer park, picking up the main drive towards Studley Roger.

If you are not a National Trust member and wish to avoid the entrance charge, turn left to reach the access road that leads to the main Visitor Centre car parks. From here a permissive path runs alongside the access road to the column of the great stone obelisk and church, from where there is an extensive view across the whole estate to Ripon, the church and drive aligned exactly with the tower of Ripon Cathedral. Head in that direction across the great deer park and along the main drive, where the path from the Water Garden entrance joins.

About 400 metres from the park entrance, between mature chestnut trees, a path heads left diagonally up a gentle slope to meet a gate in the park wall and an enclosed path to Studley Roger village. Cross the village street, keeping in the same direction, soon passing fields and a crossing of paths to meet the main B6265 less than a mile west of Ripon. Cross with care. In a few metres there is a pavement to walk along, and soon you pass a little park and Ripon Spa hotel to find your way into Yorkshire's smallest but most charming city, with its fine market place, complete with medieval horn blower, market cross and, just beyond the Market Place, magnificent cathedral. There is also a choice of pubs and cafes to sample before catching one of the frequent buses from the main bus station, reached along a side road just north of the Market Place.

Across the Nidderdale Watershed

KILNSEY TO PATELEY BRIDGE

FACT FILE

Distance: 17 miles (27 kilometres).

Maps: Harvey Dales South, East. Explorer OL2, OL30.

Terrain: The first section of the walk uses rough moorland tracks and paths, quite tough going in places, with a steady ascent to 540 metres. This area is totally exposed without any shelter or road access – do not attempt in severe weather or very low cloud. Latter part beyond Stean is on field paths and farm tracks, and is generally easy going.

Refreshment and accommodation: How Stean Gorge, café open daily, all day, food. Crown Inn Middlesmoor, open all day weekends, lunchtime weekdays. Café and pubs in Lofthouse, Ramsgill, Wath. Good choice of inns and cafes in Pateley Bridge. Youth Hostel: Kettlewell 2 miles (3km). B&B accommodation in Middlesmoor and Pateley Bridge.

Toilets: Middlesmoor, Pateley Bridge.

Transport: Outward: Weekdays service 72/74 Skipton/Ilkley to Kilnsey; Sundays 800, 805. Return: Two late afternoon buses service 25 summer Sundays only, service 24 Pateley Bridge to Harrogate hourly (Sundays two hourly), 802 to Leeds via Otley summer Sundays.

Stage point: Middlesmoor (10 miles/16km) served by service 25 – late afternoon buses on summer Sundays only, which also call at Lofthouse, Ramsgill and Wath road end.

Drivers: Summer Sundays only: Park Otley, catch 800/805 outward, return 802 to Otley; other times park Leeds and travel out by Metrotrain to Ilkley or Skipton then 72, 74 or 805, return on 24 to Harrogate then train or 36 bus to Leeds.

A cross dale walk over an ancient moorland pass linking Wharfedale and Nidderdale using a monastic packhorse route which once linked two important granges of Fountains Abbey at Malham and Kilnsey. The first part of this walk through Bycliffe and Mossdale goes through some of the remotest country in the north of England, with few signs of human habitation for around nine miles, before the gentle descent into Stean Gorge. The final section of the route from Middlesmoor in Upper Nidderdale uses part of the Nidderdale Way alongside Gouthwaite Reservoir into Pateley Bridge.

Route

From Kilnsey walk 300 metres past the Trout Farm or alight at the bus stop at Conistone Lane End. Walk over the bridge into Conistone, turning left for 200 metres along the lane to Kettlewell, passing Conistone church, to where a stony track, Scot Gate Lane, goes through a gateway. Follow the track as its climbs fairly steeply through more gates towards the television and wireless mast on Wass Hill. As you reach the rocky outcrops above Conistone Dib, you soon cross the Dales Way long distance path as it runs between Grassington and Kettlewell.

This ancient route known in various parts as Scot Gate, Bycliffe Road or Sandy Gate was for many centuries a busy packhorse way linking the western and eastern Dales. It was especially important in monastic times when it was used by the monks and lay brothers of

Fountains Abbey as a route from Mastiles Lane to Bouthwaite and over their land in Nidderdale, still known as Fountains Earth Moor, towards the parent Abbey. Between the seventeenth and nineteenth centuries the modern track provided access to the Bycliffe lead mines, and it is currently in use as an access to grouse shooting moors above Conistone.

Keep ahead on the track, which now levels out along a high plateau, entering a broad, enclosed lane, the Bycliffe Road. At the next junction of paths, keep with the stone track sharp right as it climbs uphill through Kelber Gate before bearing left again and descending into a long, shallow, treeless valley, crossing the boggy land known as Byclffe.

The valley ahead, extending northwards, forms Mossdale, one the wildest and loneliest of the smaller Yorkshire dales. The landscape all around is pockmarked with the remains of lead mining – shafts, spoil tips and areas of former activity. There are scores of caves and potholes, including Mossdale Caverns, site of a

The remote sheepfold on Aygill Beck, one of the headwaters of the River Nidd.

tragic caving disaster some years ago.

Close to the shooting hut, where there is a junction of tracks, follow the track as it turns sharp right to ford Mossdale Beck. The beck can be deep at this point, and it usually easier to ford the stream a few metres upstream. The route continues along a fainter track, indicated by a lichen-covered footpath sign, to the north of the hut. But after about 150 metres look for the fork, right, where a narrow path bears off half right, climbing across tussocky moor. It is a clear path, however, and its route along a public bridleway is marked by posts topped with blue paint.

A steep and steady climb now up the hillside, passing a line of grouse shooting butts, contouring the hillside before eventually bending uphill to the right, still on the narrow path, to the summit of the pass on the ridge at

Sandy Gate, where there is a rickety stile in the wire fence.

Sandy Gate lies on the main eastern watershed of the Dales, a saddle between the twin peaks of Great Whernside and the lonely eminence of Meugher, perhaps the remotest and least inviting summit in the Yorkshire Dales. Mossdale Beck heads south to join the River Wharfe, the seeps and dykes that emerge from the peat forming the headwaters of Stean Beck, which eventually runs east into the River Nidd. The ridge is known to this day as Friar Hood, a link with its monastic history, and now forms the boundary between the Yorkshire Dales National Park and Nidderdale Area of Outstanding Natural Beauty.

The top section of Sandy Gate is clearly visible as an ancient, metalled way across the pass. After a few metres it becomes a narrow, winding path, still clearly defined (though there is currently no waymarking). It broadly keeps around 100 metres above and to the north of Friar Hood Gill, over some steep and rough side gullies, mainly rough grass, rushes and peat, and some 100 to 200 metres north of the main Straight Stean Beck.

This is tough but exhilarating walking, the main valley now coming into view. Keep the same direction across rough pasture, over several crossing gills and boggy areas (keep to the higher places or tufts of rushes). In some places fragments of the medieval road can still be traced. At other points it is a faint narrow way between bracken.

Some 2km (about a mile) from Sandy Gate the path begins to be less distinct. Head for what seems to be a section of wooden fence straight ahead. This is in fact the top of a lovely stone sheepfold at the top of Great Blowing Gill, a side valley. Make your way round to a point below the sheepfold, where a metalled track climbs the other side of the stream.

The public right of way crosses the wall ahead and stays around 250 metres above the Yorkshire Water access road. Most walkers will be tempted to stay on the track, picking up this good valley access road. If you choose this

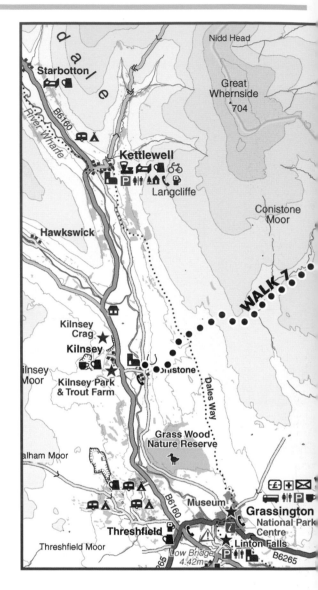

route, which is much easier to follow and causes less erosion, keep away from all reservoir structures but stay along the level, straight track as it crosses a metal bridge and heads through gates.

Follow the track for another 2km, through gates, to where, soon after the first farmhouse and barn at High Riggs becomes visible below on the right, the track curves to the right to a field gate and fork. Do not go through the gate. The public right of way now rejoins the track and follows the right hand side of the wall down to what in fact is now a derelict farmhouse.

Just past the farmhouse there is narrow

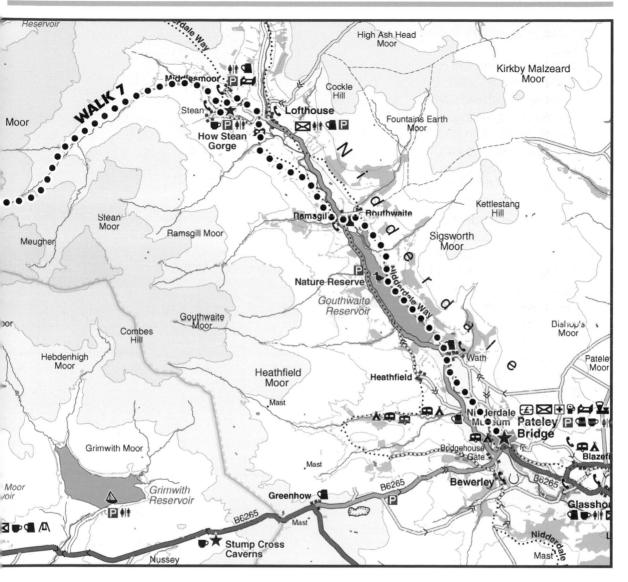

gap stile in the wall. This leads directly to the track that goes down towards Low Rigg Farm ahead. Turn right at the farm along the path, which follows a narrow tongue of land between the streams. Cross the beck at a footbridge over Armathwaite Gill and through a pretty, wooded gorge to where there is a junction of paths. Turn left sharply uphill to join the lane just south of Middlesmoor village.

Middlesmoor, with the Crown Inn and cafes and summer Sunday afternoon transport, is an excellent place for rest and refreshment before tackling the last part of the walk down Nidderdale itself. Start at the church with its

magnificent views down the dale to Gouthwaite Reservoir, before taking the path through fields down to the lane corner above Lofthouse. Turn right towards How Stean, past the car park and the track that heads towards Steam Farm, now picking up the Nidderdale Way (well waymarked) which follow a combination of tracks and field paths along the hillside past West House Farm, keeping the same direction to emerge at Ramsgill.

From Ramsgill follow the lane across the river to Bouthwaite, turning right along the track that follows the far side of the Gouthwaite Reservoir, a noted bird sanctuary celebrated for

both migrants and waders. Continue past Coville House Farm soon going close to the reservoir embankment. Keep to the narrower path past the dam and then along the riverside to Wath. From Wath there is an easy-to-follow path, through stiles, part of it on the old, long vanished Nidd Valley Light Railway trackbed, which eventually emerges into a housing estate at the edge

Gouthwaite Reservoir, now one of Yorkshire's most popular bird sanctuaries.

of Pateley Bridge. Continue straight ahead for the bus station, shops, cafes and inns of this attractive former mining and quarrying town, now rightly regarded as the capital of Nidderdale.

Over the Stake Pass to Semerwater

BUCKDEN TO HAWES

This is one of the classic walks of the Yorkshire Dales, crossing between Wharfedale and Wensleydale, in the footsteps of Julius Agricola, using the great Roman general's campaigning road over the watershed past Semerwater to his fort in Bainbridge. It then follows the Wensleydale railway line before an easy ascent to Sedbusk with panoramic views of Hawes and Wether Fell.

Route

The village of Buckden – once the site of a hunting lodge in the Plantagenet hunting forest of Upper Wharfedale and Langstrothdale – is the last settlement of any size in Wharfedale and the terminus of the Upper Wharfedale bus service. It is also a focal point of the National Trust's Wharfedale Estate, a magnificent area of woodland, fell side and pastureland in the heart of the National Park given to the National Trust by the late Graham Watson, a leading campaigner for National Parks.

The walk starts at the gate at the far end of the car park and ascends the fairly steep track, Buckden Raikes, which leads out of the village and along the shoulder of Buckden Pike. Keep straight ahead along the track, though gates eventually to join the B6160 above Cray Bridge near its waterfall – a fall which only rarely appears, in wet weather, when it can be spectacular.

Walk half a mile (1 km) up the road to the top of the pass where, at the last bend, a gate leads to a track stretching in a straight line up the slope ahead in true Roman style. This is Stake Pass, one of the many campaigning

roads build by the Julius Agricola in the first century during his conquest of Britain as a means of subduing the war-like tribes of Brigantia – modern Yorkshire – by creating a

FACT FILE

Distance: 15 miles (24 kilometres).

Maps: Harvey Dales South, North. OS OL 30.

Terrain: Mainly stony tracks, over moorland; short sections of lake and riverside paths, some field paths and short road sections. Some moderate ascents, but generally fairly easy going

Refreshment and accommodation: Rose & Crown, Bainbridge – open daily, all day, food. Café, shop in Bainbridge. Choice of cafes, pubs, B&Bs in Hawes. Youth Hostels in Kettlewell and Hawes.

Toilets: Buckden, Bainbridge, Hawes

Transport: Outward: Weekdays: Dales Bus 72 service from Skipton to Buckden (connection with 74 from Ilkley at Grassington). Sundays and Bank Holidays: 800/805 direct from Leeds and Ilkley. Return: Weekdays: Hawes Village bus 113 to Garsdale station for trains to Skipton. Sundays and Bank Holidays: 800, 805 to Ilkley and Leeds

Stage point: Bainbridge (10 miles) by catching service 156 or 157 into Hawes, or (Sundays) 800, 805 back to Buckden and Ilkley. NB: Walk can also be shortened on Sundays by 2 miles (3km) and some road walking and climbing eliminated by catching 800 or 805 bus to alight at start of Stake Pass track, on top of Kidstones Pass.

Drivers: Weekdays: Park Skipton and catch service 72 to return on 113 bus and train to Skipton. Sundays: Park Grassington or Buckden and use 800, 805.

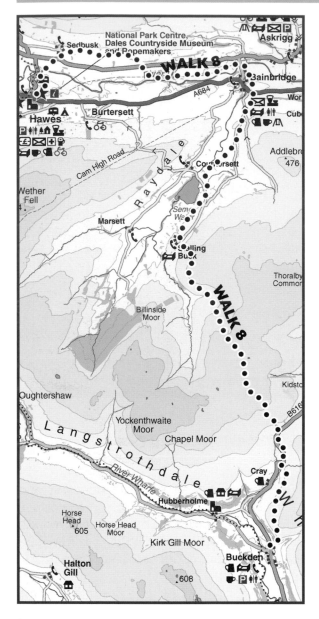

Peaks to the west.

The track levels at the summit of the path and crosses the open moorland of Stake Moss. Soon after it becomes enclosed between walls, a ladder stile on the left by a field gate indicates the footpath over Great Silky Top to Shaw Gate, which, though it is shorter than the main track, crosses rough moorland and a steep gill. This inevitably takes longer, but if there are motor vehicles around over Stake Pass or you welcome a change of terrain, it is worth taking. Otherwise the main track curves westwards, past the junction with the track over Stake Allotment to Thoralby (another fine walk), curving round past Bank Wood, with Semerwater finally coming into view.

As Stalling Busk comes into view below you, take the narrow track, Bob Lane, which swings left down to this delightful hamlet. Go through the village to pick up the path down to Stalling Busk's gaunt ruined church. Built in 1603 and restored in 1722 it was abandoned in 1909 for a more conveniently situated chapel in the village; a century's neglect has resulted in its picturesque decay.

The path continues along the edge of Semerwater, one of the loveliest and the largest of all Yorkshire's natural lakes, covering some 60 acres. It is an ancient glacial lake, rich in history and legend. Most notable is the celebrated medieval ballad relating the sudden drowning of the valley after a terrible storm, which caused the deaths of all the inhabitants of the nearby village with the exception of an elderly couple who gave shelter to a travelling beggar. The lake's creation was not quite so instantaneous being glacial meltwater trapped behind the great moraine that blocked Raydale after the last Ice Age. The lakeside was later inhabited by Iron Age people attracted by the fishing. Perhaps in distant folk memory this was the legend of the doomed village. It is a notable wildlife sanctuary, a breeding area for great crested grebe and tufted duck and a wide variety of migrant birds. Fish in the lake include roach, perch, bream trout and eel. Though all the views of Semerwater are fine,

fast means of communication to bring well disciplined troops to trouble spots.

The old road has remained for centuries as a way for horses and wagons, and still has vehicular rights, so expect to see the occasional 4x4 or motorcyclist. Thankfully, as it has a mainly hard surface, there are relatively few areas of bad vehicle erosion. It is an easy, steady gradient, with, in clear weather, ever more spectacular views of the fells as you climb. Buckden Pike is behind you and there are glimpses of Fountains Fell and the Three

the most dramatic of all are to be enjoyed when you reach the lane at the farm, and continue to the head of the lake by the great Carlow Stone. This is a boulder allegedly dropped here by the Devil, but less romantically one of several carried from higher land by the retreating glacier and deposited as the ice melted. The magnificent view to the surrounding fells above Raydale were captured in dramatic style by JMW Turner, England's greatest painter, when he toured the Dales in 1816. Engravings or reproductions from the original watercolour are constantly to be seen.

The little River Bain, reputedly England's shortest river at just under two miles long, drains from the northern tip of Semerwater. A stile at the bridge leads to a path alongside the river that eventually leaves it to climb Bracken Hill. This glacial moraine still blocks the valley, with the River Bain carving its energetic way through a narrow gorge below.

There is an excellent view of the site of the Roman fort of Virosidium, built by Agricola in

Semerwater on a still winter's day.

AD80 as a wooden stockade on earth and stone foundations. A campaigning fort where his legions could rest on the long march north from the fort at Olicana (Ilkley), it is now perceptible as straight lines and faint ridges on the hillside ahead.

You reach the outskirts of Bainbridge by the bridge and waterfall, from where a short walk brings you into this most delightful of Dales villages with its magnificent green, lovely old houses, stocks, old water mill and ancient inn. Every night, between All Hallows (November 1st) and Shrovetide, the horn kept at the inn is still sounded to direct benighted travellers from the surrounding hills, a relic of the days well before motor traffic when Bainbridge was a settlement of a dozen cottages in the great hunting Forest of Wensleydale.

The route follows the Askrigg road out of the village, over the bridge across the River Ure

Spring always comes late to the upper dales – Abbotside Common in snow.

where a stile on the left accesses a path that climbs the pasture to reach and follow the trackbed of the Wensleydale railway. This once vital trans-Pennine lifeline through the dale between Northallerton to Garsdale was closed to passengers in 1954 and for freight in 1964, but now, thanks to the Wensleydale Railway Association, has been reopened for regular trains between Leeming Bar and Redmire. Hopefully it will soon to link back into Northallerton and eventually reach Aysgarth, Hawes and even Garsdale.

Follow the railway trackbed through stiles until it eventually reaches a narrow back lane past Cams House and Old Cam farms, where a path marked for Litherskew reaches the Askrigg road by an old quarry. It continues in the same direction towards the hamlet of Litherskew. Just below this hamlet it joins a nar-row lane, from where there are extensive views across and to the head of the dale, with the massive shape of Wether Fell dominating the background and Hawes with its distinctive church tower soon visible below.

Continue to Sedbusk, from where a choice of paths leads down across the fields, across the lane to a lovely little packhorse bridge over a beck and into Brunt Acres Road where its meets the Pennine Way. Look for a narrow path left which avoids the road, running along the riverbank between the two bridges, and then on the right a paved causeway that leads to the outskirts of Hawes.

Hawes – its name meaning a gap or pass through the hills – is an unpretentious little market town (market day Tuesday) with lots of good places to eat, drink, shop, stay overnight or spend a weekend. The National Park Centre and excellent Dales Countryside Museum – and main bus terminus – are on your left, with most pubs, cafes shops and Youth Hostel on the right.

The Old Kendal Road

SKIPTON TO SETTLE

The Aire Gap is generally considered to be the southern boundary of the Yorkshire Dales. This natural, relatively low level pass between Airedale and Ribblesdale has been a vital transport corridor since prehistoric times, and with turnpike road (now modern trunk road), canal and railway, is still one of the most important east-west routes through the Pennines. This walk follows even older roads for most of the way, picking up part of the old pre-turnpike highway to Kendal. Until the Keighley-Kendal turnpike road was built in the eighteenth century, this was the route used by the carriers' carts and pack-horse trains which once linked the busy manufacturing town of Kendal with the thriving market town of Leeds, from where textiles and manufactured goods could be shipped along the navigable River Aire to east coast ports and mainland Europe.

Route

Start the walk along the Leeds-Liverpool canal towpath, accessed from Skipton bus station across the footbridge over the canal to the towpath. From the rail station, cross from the main entrance to reach the canal along the road into Aireville Park to the right of Magnet Joinery.

The 127-mile Leeds-Liverpool canal, built in stages between 1770 and 1812, remains one of the most impressive achievements of the canal age. As the many surviving canal side mills testify – many of them now converted to offices or dwellings – the canal gave an enormous boost to industry in Skipton, and indeed across the entire Pennines, carrying the coal, limestone, wool, cotton and other raw materials that fuelled the Industrial Revolution. Follow the towpath for approximately two miles (2.5 from the bus station), including a short length of path alongside the main road, to where the second concrete road bridge, carrying the A59, comes into view. About 200 metres before the bridge a gap in the wall on the left (about 50 metres

FACT FILE

Distance: 16 miles (25 kilometres).

Maps: Harvey Dales South; OS Explorer OL2.

Terrain: The first section follows the Leeds-Liverpool canal towpath, then field paths to Gargrave. From here tracks and a short section of lane are followed to the outskirts of Settle. There are steady climbs, the second, over Hellifield Moor, more extended.

Refreshment and accommodation: Popular Dalesman café and two inns in Gargrave. Choice of inns and cafes in Settle. B&B in Gargrave and Settle.

Toilets: Skipton, Gargrave, Settle.

Transport: Outward: Regular Metro electric trains Leeds/Bradford-Skipton, or X84 from Ilkley, Otley, Leeds.

Return: Frequent train service Settle-Hellifield-Skipton-Leeds (some calling at Gargrave), Sunday service more limited. Pennine Bus operates hourly Settle to Skipton via Hellifield and Gargrave (two hourly Saturdays and no service Sundays).

Stage points: Gargrave (5 miles, 8km); Hellifield (12 miles,19km) with bus and train service back to Skipton as above.

Drivers: Park Skipton, return by train or bus from Settle,

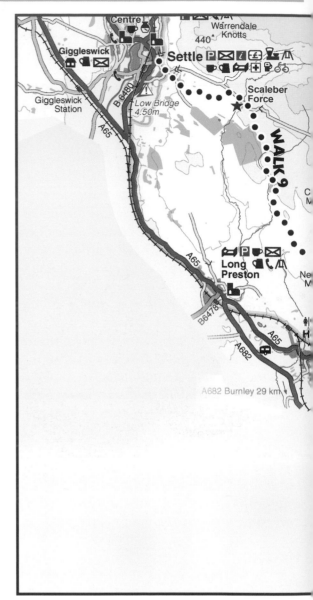

Mark House Lane, Gargrave – the old Kendal road before the modern turnpike, now the A65, was built.

before a wooden bench) leads to a path joining a track to the main A6069 from Skipton.

Cross the road with care and walk on the verge wherever possible for 150 metres to where, at a lay-by, a well-used path (not shown on most maps) leads over the disused stone bridge over the river. Continue to the main A59. Cross with care and opposite and straight ahead you will see a stone stile and footpath sign. This leads to a path across a large open pasture. Keep ahead with the direction of the sign to a low stone wall and wooden stile by trees ahead. The path keeps the same direction to the top left-hand corner of the next huge pasture, then alongside the wall for another 400 metres, before turning sharp right to an arched underpass under the railway line.

The path now follows the railway embank-

ment. Keep ahead with waymarks through gate and stiles, going close to the railway before bearing slightly right. Follow a line of mature trees, heading towards Gargrave church past Kirk Sink – the site of a Roman village – to join a farm track into Gargrave village.

Gargrave is a former coaching village with extensive riverside village green, a fifteenth century church (the last resting place of Sir Ian Macleod, Chancellor of the Exchequer in the Heath Government), two excellent inns and the celebrated Dalesman Café that always wel-

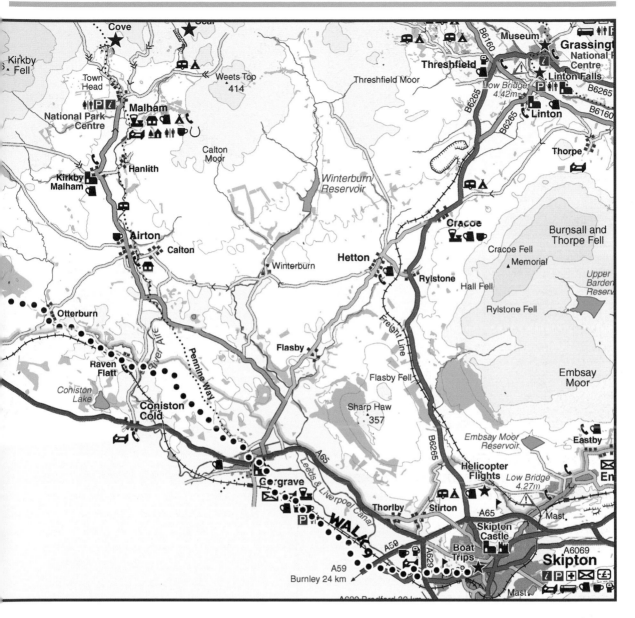

comes walkers and cyclists. It is also a key staging point on the Pennine Way, and one possibility of this walk is to divert along the Pennine Way for six miles to Malham.

The route from Gargrave actually follows the Pennine Way along West Street and over the canal, bearing westwards along what soon becomes an attractive stony way. Leave the Pennine Way as it heads northwards and continue along the lane past Harrows Laithe. This is Mark House Lane, once part of the old Kendal road. You are now climbing one of the

first of several of the Craven 'drumlins', mounds of glacial waste that form the characteristic hillocks, a dominant feature of this part of the Dales, with increasingly extensive views as you climb.

The track descends to join the lane at Bell Busk. Cross at the junction and head along the lane towards Otterburn, past Raven Flatt. Bell Busk almost certainly gained its name from a long vanished medieval inn – Busk or Bush being the traditional sign for an inn, and Bell its individual symbol – the Bell Inn, though an

Otherwise keep ahead over somewhat badly eroded tracks to where a gate above the brow of the hill leads into a lane, the surface gradually improving. This is Langber Lane, one of the loveliest old ways in Craven, winding its way through natural gaps between the drumlins, climbing past Bookilber Barn and a pretty woodland, Langber Plantation, now owned and managed by the Woodland Trust and accessible to the public.

Langber Lane continues up to the strangely named Wild Share plantation before finally emerging in the lane from Airton 150 metres before Scaleber Bridge. At the bridge take time to explore Scaleber Force, a delightful waterfall, reached by steps and a narrow path on the left just 50 metres beyond the bridge, a hidden jewel of a fall in its own deep, wooded gill.

Return to High Hill Lane, with magnificent, panoramic views of the great cliffs and scars ahead, marking the line of the Craven Fault. About 100 metres past the junction with Stockdale Lane, take the track, left, known as Lambert Lane, which heads between fields. After 200 metres go over the stile on the right, leading to a path which follows the field wall, soon descending and passing a small reservoir into Mitchell Lane above Upper Settle.

You are soon on the outskirts of Settle, its clusters of stone cottages perched along the hillside as you descend into its narrow streets and courts, past the extraordinary Jacobean house, now a museum, known as The Folly, the fine market place with its 1820s French-style Town Hall and celebrated Shambles. If you have planned your walk well there will be ample time to visit the shops, cafes and pubs of this most delightful of Dales market towns, before taking the Settle-Carlisle line train or Pennine bus back to Skipton.

actual bell on a building in the hamlet (that still survives) once summoned workers to the small local textile mill. Follow the lane to Otterburn alongside the little River Aire, the drumlin on the road overlooking the lane significantly named Kendal Hill.

In Otterburn turn sharp left, back along the opposite site of Otterburn Beck, to pick up, right, the start of a long green track, Dacre Lane. Once again this is the old Kendal road – steady walking now, gradually gaining height past Wenningber Plantation onto Hellifield Moor. Where the path enters open moorland past the end of the wood, keep straight ahead along vehicle tracks through gates to Hellifield Moor Top. If you are breaking your journey at Hellifield, a broad, scarcely defined path heads left to a gate some 400 metres over the crest of the hill. This marks the start of Haw Lane, a track leading for just over a mile into Hellifield with its railway station, inn and bus stops.

Along the Craven Fault

SETTLE TO GRASSINGTON

This classic ramble joins three Dales – Ribblesdale, Malhamdale and Wharfedale – closely following the spectacular line of the Craven Fault which divides the dark gritstone and boulder clay lands of South Craven from the paler, limestone country to the north. This fault was a profound shifting of the earth's crust, exposing underlying Carboniferous limestones, which have weathered into the dramatic pale crags and scars that make such a feature on this walk. But this is a ramble which is, for observant walkers, equally as rich in archaeological and historic features.

Route

From Settle Market Place follow the lane which starts from the north-east corner Constitution Hill, soon climbing up and behind the last cottages of the town, becoming a stony track. About 50 metres beyond the last gate, the path to Stackhouses (not visible on the ground) turns off at right angles, climbing steeply up open pasture. Keep the same direction up a long narrow pasture to alongside the next wall before crossing to the next stile in the opposite wall corner, soon descending a shallow, dry valley, with the spectacular limestone scar formation of Warrendale Knotts and Attermire Scar to your left. Over more stiles the path follows the wall on the right before reaching the top of Stockdale lane at a gate. Along the farm road, but before the farm, the path climbs up behind the buildings and becomes a green track ascending a narrow natural pass with Rye Loaf Hill on the right.

This was once the main route between Settle and Malham, used by William Wordsworth when he travelled this way from Malham to Settle by carrier's cart in the 1790s. At the summit of the pass, on Pikedaw Hill, with grand views of Malham Tarn and surrounding fells to the left, you pass former calamine (zinc ore) mineshafts, once hugely busy in the eighteenth and nineteenth centuries. At the third gate, where the track starts to descend, some 150 metres ahead is the base

---

FACT FILE

Distance: 17 miles (27 kilometres).

Maps: Harvey Dales South; Explorer OL2.

Terrain: Moorland tracks and field paths across pasture. Some steep sections, but generally moderate.

Refreshment and accommodation: Buck Inn or Lister's Arms, Malham. Several cafes in Malham – Youth Hostel and B&Bs in the village. Old Hall Inn, Threshfield; choice of pubs, cafes and B&Bs in Grassington.

Toilets: Settle, Malham, Grassington.

Transport: Outward: Regular trains daily to Settle from Leeds and Skipton; weekday Pennine Bus service (hourly or two hourly). Return: Hourly buses 72/67A from Grassington to Skipton (daily), two hourly weekdays to Ilkley (74) 800, 805 to Ilkley and Leeds Sundays.

Stage point: Malham (7 miles – 11km), with infrequent bus to Skipton – late afternoon only weekdays, but every two hours on Saturdays and summer Sundays (280).

Drivers: Park Skipton take the train or bus to Settle, return on 72 or 67A from Grassington or Threshfield.

(Opposite) Janet's Foss pool and waterfall create a magical moment on any walk to Gordale.
(This page) Gordale Scar with its magnificent entrance is one of the most impressive limestone features anywhere in the British Isles.

of Nappa Cross, with a modern shaft. It is one of the many monastic boundary crosses to be found in the Malham area, mainly to delineate the often-disputed boundaries between land owned by the Cistercians of Fountains Abbey and the Augustinians of Bolton Priory.

The track descends past Fair Sleets Gate eventually reaching the Cove Road, almost opposite Malham Cove. Turn right down the steep lane for some 300 metres, but where the lane bends sharp left keep straight ahead through the gate along Long Lane. This track curves round behind and eventually into the invariably busy Malham village, where most people will choose to pause for well earned refreshment.

The next stage of the walk follows the Pennine Way to the far side of Malham Beck, passing three fields before turning sharp left at a junction of paths through kissing gates, and then over stiles alongside Gordale Beck to Wedber Wood. At the end of the wood is Janet's Foss, a delightful curtain of water contained within its own natural bowl of tufa, bedrock and trees, complete with a small cave.

Continue right, into Gordale Lane, taking time to walk the few hundred metres to visit Gordale Scar. For over two centuries, since the days of the early Romantic poets and artists, this has been one of the wonders of the Yorkshire Dales, an awe-inspiring collapsed cavern, complete with waterfall, which has created an atmospheric narrow gorge. With its

One of several mysterious Bronze Age 'ring cairns' or stone circles in the Dales, the one above Bordley enjoys a magnificent land-scape setting.

scree slopes, ravens and yew trees, it is a place that never loses its appeal.

Return to Hawthorn Lane, quickly losing the crowds and the cars as you climb steeply out of the valley, with its rich pattern of field walls and earthworks, many dating from pre-historic times. After just over half a mile (almost a kilometre), as the gradient levels, take the stony track right that climbs to Weets Cross. Though the way to Bordley is over a stile some 120 metres north of Weets Top, it is worth climbing up to this monastic boundary cross on the hilltop, as it is a superb viewpoint.

Return to where the stile leads to a path over rough pasture, heading due eastwards. Go towards and through a little scrubby pinewood ahead, over stiles, the path bearing southwards to Park House farm. Head between the farmhouse and barn (look for waymarks) to follow the far side of the wall to the north of the farm. Pass through gates that take the path in front of the barn past Bleak Bank, dropping down open pasture where, to the left of Low Laithe, a stile leads to a track that descends to Bordley Beck. Turn left to follow the path leading over a ford and little footbridges to Bordley Hall Farm, but immediately through the gate before the farm, follow the wall left and uphill. Keeping the same direction, cross stiles towards the tiny hamlet of Bordley.

The path goes between the farm buildings and through cattle gates to reach the lane through the hamlet. Turn right past the two farms that constitute the hamlet, but sharp right after 50 metres to locate the path alongside the wall, signed Threshfield, that dips into a dry valley, over a stile and then up the hillside ahead. You may want to visit the remarkable Bordley Circle, just before you reach limestone outcrops and a small limekiln above. Head due north on a track for some 400 metres to a point close to a wall (marked as a cairn on the map), where this small Bronze Age circle commands an impressive view of the surrounding hills. (This area is now part of the Open Country under the CROW Act 2000 where access is usually permitted).

The tiny farming hamlet of Bordley is one of the most isolated communities in the Yorkshire Dales.

Return to the right of way, which climbs through a fascinating area of limestone outcrops and old, complex enclosures. Stiles mark the way through several of these small enclosures, as the path descends to Height Laithe, where it follows the enclosed track to your right. Go first left at the junction, heading towards Cow Close Wood, a lovely stretch of limestone woodland, passing Height House, into an area of scattered trees and pasture, dotted with primroses in spring.

The path, now well defined, goes through the centre of Wood Nook caravan site. Follow the lane from the entrance towards Skirethorns, but keep ahead at the junction for 250 metres to pass Grysedale House where a path, left, heads over a stile down to the shallow valley formed by Rowley and Spiredale Becks. You cross an access bridge over the stream, then bear right through more stiles, eventually taking the signposted way into and across a large field, at the far corner of which a stile leads to a path behind the Old Hall Inn in Threshfield.

Cross the extremely busy B6265 and continue past the village green to the Burnsall road, going right for a few metres to where a gate gives access to the bridleway down to Threshfield's Elizabethan primary school. Left here along the lane for 150 metres to where a path, right, leads along the riverside to the footbridge over Linton Falls, another spectacular feature created by the Craven Fault. The enclosed paved footpath, locally known as the Snake Walk, takes you to the Transport Interchange and National Park Centre, and on into the centre of Grassington.

Malham Tarn and the Monks' Road

HELLIFIELD TO BUCKDEN

Another fine cross-dale walk through the limestone heartland of the central Dales, linking Hellifield on the Settle-Carlisle line with Upper Wharfedale, taking in some of *the grandest scenery of Malhamdale and Littondale in the process.*

Route

From Hellifield station follow Station Road down to the A65. Turn left, crossing at refuge, and going under the railway bridge to recross at the pedestrian lights (NB toilets on right). Almost opposite the church turn left along Haw Grove, which leads into Haw Lane, over the level crossing, becoming an enclosed bridlepath that climbs gradually between the Craven drumlins. It leads to a large open pasture to the west of Wenningber Hill. Head just to the right of the line of woodland ahead, bearing right towards trees where you'll pick up the line of Dacre Lane, the old green road to Settle (see walk 9). Turn right through the gate and along the enclosed way through Wenningber Plantation, climbing the low hill known as Crossber before descending into the hamlet of Otterburn.

Go left to the top of the hamlet to pick up the path through the imposing gates of Grange House Farm – this looks like a private garden but as the sign indicates it carries a public path. Immediately beyond the courtyard, a stony track alongside Otterburn Beck is picked up. After 700 metres a gate in the wall on the right (with signpost) indicates the footpath, which now bears right along a green way climbing uphill, through gates and stiles, to the right of the wood ahead. It continues across broad pasture to cross the lane from Airton at stiles, the path signed to Kirkby Malham. Keep ahead up Warber Hill, alongside a wall and by a wood, following waymarks, fingerposts and stiles, over

FACT FILE

Distance: 20 miles (32 kilometres).

Maps: Harvey Dales South; OS Explorer OL2, OL30.

Terrain: Farm tracks and field paths across pasture. Some steep sections, especially in the Malham area, and between Litton and Buckden, making this a fairly strenuous day's walking, which can easily be split by using available public transport to and from Malham or by staying overnight in Malham.

Refreshment and accommodation: Café at Hellifield station; Victoria Inn Kirkby Malham; Buck Inn or Lister's Arms, Malham. Several cafes and B&Bs in Malham. Falcon Inn, Arncliffe; Queen's Head, Litton; café, shop and Buck Inn, Buckden. Youth Hostels in Malham and Kettlewell village.

Toilets: Hellifield, Malham, Buckden, Kettlewell.

Transport: Outward: Regular trains from Skipton (Leeds-Settle or Leeds-Morecambe lines), weekday Pennine Bus service (hourly or two hourly). Return: Weekdays late afternoon buses 72/74 from Buckden or Kettlewell to Ilkley or Skipton; 800, 805 to Ilkley on Sundays

Stage point: Malham (7 miles, 11km) with infrequent bus to Skipton – late afternoon only weekdays, two hourly Saturdays and summer Sundays (280/804); Kettlewell (via Old Cote Moor), 16.5 miles – 26km), return bus as above.

Drivers: Park Skipton and take the train or bus to Hellifield, return on 72, 805 or 67A from Buckden or Kettlewell via Grassington.

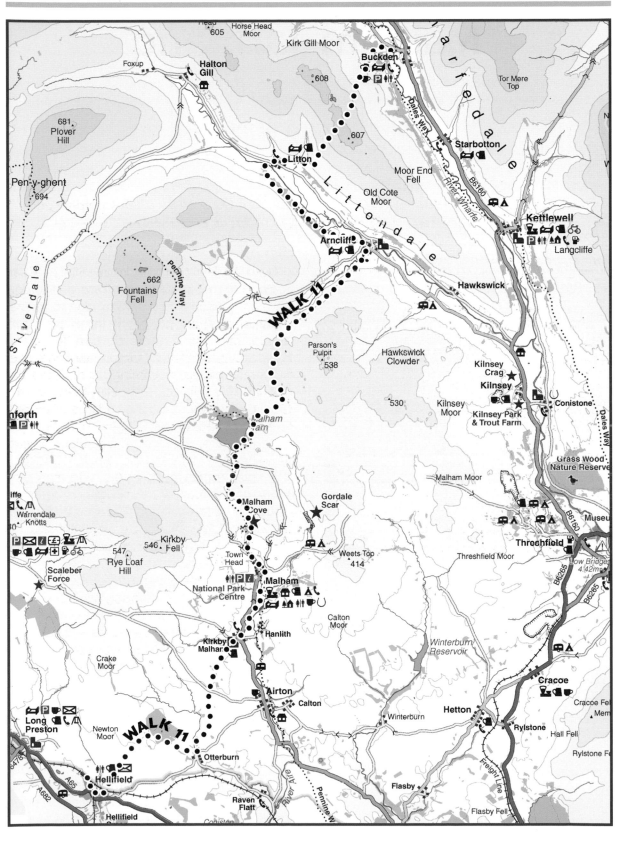

a tiny footbridge and another hillock before dropping into the next shallow valley. The tower of Kirkby Malham church is now visible, the path curving down steps to cross a footbridge.

It is worth pausing at Kirkby Malham's fifteenth century church, a fine example or Perpendicular style, with a Norman font and some remarkable carved stone heads. Otherwise go to the cross roads past the Victoria Inn to the lane down towards Malham, taking the tarmac access road upstream from Hanlith Bridge, the path going around the outside and along the attractive mills ponds of the former Scalegill Mill. Keep ahead past Airehead Springs – the source of the River Aire – into Malham.

For most people Malham with its National

The descent to Kirkby Malham with its fine fifteenth century church.

Park centre and refreshment facilities will be worth a break, with the opportunity to divide the walk into a shorter seven and thirteen miles stages at this point, with return buses to Skipton (daily except winter Sundays) but also a choice of overnight accommodation and refreshment to make it a weekend walk.

The onward route is the obvious popular walk northwards out of the village along the Pennine Way, taking the Cove Road and the invariably busy path to the magnificent Cove. Climb the polished limestone steps to the left of the Cove to the great summit pavement, to the rear of which the Pennine Way continues along Watlowes, a spectacular dry valley through a rocky gorge. Like the Cove, it is limestone scenery at its most magnificent, the valley scoured out by a long vanished watercourse. Climb to the steep head of the gorge, to the stile, turning right across the scar, climbing out of the ravine and along the wallside past Water Sinks to the car park at Malham Tarn. Walk across straight ahead to the little dam at the end of the Tarn.

The Tarn is a natural lake, a geological curiosity with, thanks to complex faulting, underlying impervious Silurian rocks capturing water in otherwise dry limestone country, though its level was artificially raised by the creation of the dam in the late eighteenth century. Malham Tarn House directly ahead was built as a country house by Walter Morrison, local philanthropist, in the middle of the last century. It is now the Field Studies Centre, where high-level environmental courses are taught and research is carried out by the Field Studies Council. Tarn Moor to the west of the Centre is an internationally important Nature Reserve – access is by permit only.

Follow the path around the woodland to join the main track into the Tarn House Estate. At the gate leading into the main estate, a signpost indicates a path climbing steeply back up to the right, up the wide pasture of Great Close. Follow this path through stiles, soon turning northwards away from Middle House Farm towards Middle House, an abandoned

farmhouse now cared for by the National Trust who own and protect much of the countryside around and above Malham.

You are now on the Monk's Road, as the name implies a medieval road dating from the time of the great monastic estates and network of granges owned and managed by the monks of Fountains Abbey and (in Malham) their rivals, the friars of Bolton Priory. This was the main route between extensive monastic estates in Malham and Littondale. Keep on the main path, as it curves gradually to your right over Malham Moor, a rich and complex landscape full of limestone outcrops and paving, and remains of ancient settlement. The path becomes fairly distinct as it begins a spectacular descent above Yew Bottom Scar with wonderful views into Littondale, picking its way through crags finally to descend into a track that leads directly into Arncliffe behind the Falcon Inn. This is one of the loveliest of all

Malham Cove this natural limestone cliff along the Great Scar limestone of the Mid Craven Fault was created by a gigantic primeval waterfall.

Dales villages, mercifully unspoiled with its huge village green.

If time is short, the most direct way to Kettlewell for a bus (allow at least one hour) is to cross the green and go down the lane to the church, then picking up the riverside path which cuts the corner off to cross the Hawkswick lane. Continue on a steep but steady climb through Byre Bank Wood, and then through Park Scar on a steep path that is almost a scramble. Join the popular and well-used path due east, over Old Cote Moor and the watershed on the peaty moorland summit, before the sharp and steep descent into Kettlewell.

This shorter route misses the joy of the

Arncliffe - one of the most attractive and most photographed villages of the Dales.

Littondale paths, but you need well over two hours for the full route from here to Buckden via Litton. It is reached by following the lane westwards from the green to the bridge over Cowside Beck, continuing along the farm track past New Barn that becomes a field path. This is an easy-to-follow, valley bottom path, its line marked by gates and stiles with some way-marking, with fine views to each side. It goes through Scoska Wood Nature Reserve and onto Gildersbank, following the banks of the pretty little River Skirfare, eventually passing East Garth farm for the footbridge into Litton.

Smaller than Arncliffe, Litton gives its name to the dale and is distinguished by a pub that brews it own ale. The attractions of the little inn might be tempered by the fact that the bridlepath to Buckden, which starts just east of the pub, is a long steady slog. Starting along a green way, it dips across Crystal Beck before the serious business begins. It is a hard climb – especially after eighteen miles or so – as you gain precious height, increasingly rewarded as you ascend Ackerley Moor by superb views, especially of Fountains Fell and Pen y Ghent at the head of the dale.

The path flattens out over the peat hags of Old Cote Moor, before the long and some-times boggy descent over Birks Fell, eventually joining the track above Redmire Farm down into the Langstrothdale road west of Buckden. If you've timed it well there will be opportunity to visit the village café, shop or Buck Inn, the bus most safely caught (some buses start from the car park and some do not) from the tradi-tional stop outside the Buck Inn.

Walden

KETTLEWELL TO AYSGARTH

Walden, the little tributary valley of the Ure above West Burton, is special both in not having 'dale' in its ancient name – meaning a forested area – but also in terms of road transport being a cul-de-sac valley, only accessible from the south across its dale head by foot or on horseback. This classic walk crosses the watershed from either Kettlewell or Starbotton in Wharfedale, following the ancient packhorseway known as Walden Road and going over the shoulder of Buckden Pike. It then picks its way across some wild countryside, before following an idyllic route along lanes and footpaths across flower-rich meadows to the pretty village of West Burton and linking field paths to Aysgarth. However this is a walk over some fairly wild country and should only be attempted on a reasonably clear day.

Route

If you are starting the walk from Kettlewell, walk back across the bridge to pick up the Dales Way footpath along the western side of the river – an easy, clearly marked path that reaches the footbridge over the river into Starbotton. Follow the back lane through the village, ignoring the first bridlepath on the right, continuing to the lane corner where a steep track, the start of the Walden Road up Starbotton Moor, commences. From Starbotton the lane to the left of the pub and bus stop leads to the start of the track in the lane corner.

The track, concreted in its first few metres, zigzags up the hillside steeply above the village, soon giving fine views down the valley,

FACT FILE

Distance: 13 miles (21 kilometres).

Maps: Harvey Dales South; OS Explorer OL30.

Terrain: The first section is dominated by stony and grassy tracks, with a long, steep ascent of some 470 metres – about 1,500 feet – with a similar descent into the Walden valley, then much easier terrain through a series of meadows.

Refreshment and accommodation: Fox & Hounds inn in Starbotton and also in West Burton. Palmers Flatt inn and café in Aysgarth (Falls area). B&B in Aysgarth. Youth Hostels: Kettlewell; YHA Bunkhouse at Thoralby (3km from Aysgarth).

Toilets: Kettlewell, Aysgarth.

Transport: This walk is best accomplished on a summer Sunday or Bank Holiday when the earlier and later Dales Bus 800/805 services operate between Leeds, Ilkley, Grassington, Kettlewell and Aysgarth. Outward: Catch the 800/805 to Kettlewell or Starbotton (a Starbotton start reduces the walk by 2 miles – 3.5km). Return: 800/805 from Aysgarth Falls Corner or from the road junction between Aysgarth and West Burton village (1 mile – 2km shorter).

Transport – Weekdays: Outward: Service 72/74 from Ilkley or Skipton to Kettlewell/Starbotton. Return: 156 from Aysgarth Memorial to Hawes, then 113 to Garsdale station for train to Skipton, Leeds; or 156/157 buses via Northallerton.

Stage point: West Burton (12 miles) – note service 800 leaves from main road by junction below village, but 156 from the bus stop in the village centre below Fox & Hounds.

Drivers: Sundays: Park Grassington to catch outward service 800/805 and return; weekdays park Skipton, out on 72, back on Settle-Carlisle train as above.

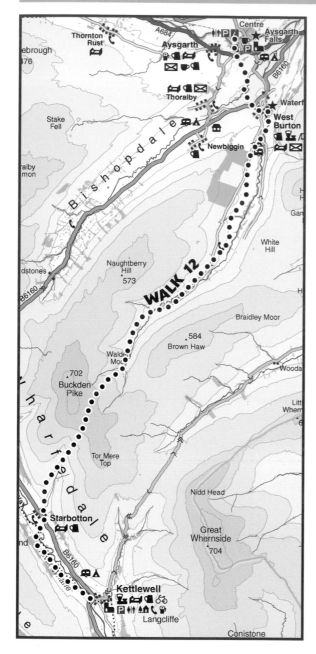

The bronze fox head on the Buckden Pike memorial that recalls a heroic tale of wartime survival.

before curving to the right and settling down to a steady climb out of Cam Gill. Keep ahead on the main track at a junction of paths, climbing steadily up, through gates, as the track thins to a single, stony way up the shoulder of the valley side above Cam Gill. You eventually enter open moorland, the gradient steepening as you climb over boggy sections of moor up and over the shoulder of Buckden Pike to the end of the summit ridge.

At the gate on the summit, it is worth leaving the main path to follow the well-used path on the far side of the wall for 400 metres towards the summit of Buckden Pike. At the end of the summit ridge you will see a stone cross. This little memorial cross with a tiny fox's head in the base commemorates the tragic, yet inspiring events of January 30th, 1942 when an RAF Wellington bomber, with a crew of Polish airman fighting with their British allies, crashed on Buckden Pike in a snowstorm. One man, Sergeant Joseph Fusniak, survived, thanks to following the footprints of a fox that led him to a point on the Pike where he could see the lights of the hamlet of Cray, from where local people rescued him.

Return to the main path. This is now a beautiful route, marked by wooden posts, which contours the summit ridge, with magnificent views to the east to Great Whernside, Little Whernside and the half-hidden valley that contains Scar House and Angram Reservoirs and the upper waters of the Nidd.

Starbotton village seen from the ancient road to Walden.

Further north the intensely green and fertile valley of Walden opens out in front of you into the distance. Harley Hill and the whaleback shape of Pen Hill are in the background and the intimate valley, dotted with farms, woods and barns, sharply contrasts with the brown expanse of Walden Moor immediately below you. It is important to keep to the path here as there are some fairly deep peat hags on all sides, even though this is newly opened CROW Act Access land (dogs not permitted off rights of way).

Follow the path as it bears gradually to the right, turning sharply right with the well defined tracks, and wooden posts, to descend steeply down Walden Moor to a relatively new shooting track below. Left along here for some 400 metres to where, on the right, the track –again well marked on the ground and with wooden posts – leads steeply down the breast of the fellside. Aim for a confluence of two narrow valleys ahead by a ruined sheepfold – a good sheltered spot if you plan a lunch stop.

Follow the stream towards the small wood ahead, the path keeping to the left of the stream. This has recently been designated a public right of way and will be appearing on any new maps. Entering the wood at a stile, you then go through a series of small enclosures, rather wet underfoot. You eventually emerge at gates to the right of Walden Head Farm and onto the cul-de-sac lane into Walden itself, a lovely fertile valley.

Follow the narrow road, Temple Lane, which is virtually traffic free, for a mile (1.5km) ignoring the first path on the right. Cross the bridge over Walden Beck, ignoring a farm drive and climbing the lane to where a second path, along the western side of the valley, commences at a stile.

This is a fine path, level, fairly well defined and waymarked, which crosses meadowland

(Above) Flower-rich spring meadow above Bridge End Farm, Walden.
(Left) West Burton village green with its unusual market cross.

for three miles to Cote Bridge. Please keep in single file through these beautiful, herb-rich hay meadows. The path, marked by stiles, is basically in a straight line, above Bridge End Farm and Hargill farm, leaving the farm track behind at Cowstone Gill, where an unofficial diversion takes you along the fence and a long series of meadows and pastures to Cote Bridge. Turn right in the lane over the bridge immediately beyond which a gate, left, leads to the beckside path. Ignoring the footbridge, bear slightly right to the stiles in the hillock above, to a path leading past the barns known as Riddings and through two more fields before turning sharp left into an enclosed way. This emerges at the small but spectacular West Burton Waterfall, perhaps better known as Cauldron Force, where Walden Beck, white and foaming, flows

into a deep, peat-brown pool.

Follow the main track to West Burton village with its attractive green, characteristic market cross (cattle and sheep fairs were once held on the green) and hospitable Fox & Hounds inn – with accommodation.

Allow at least half an hour for the walk to Aysgarth. Take the main road out of the village but as it bends right look for a narrow passageway on the left, which leads to an enclosed path down to the B6160. Cross, continuing on the path ahead, which enters open fields before turning sharp right to Eshington Bridge. Cross the bridge and almost immediately on

Aysgarth Falls in spate after spring rain.

the left a stile marks the start of a well signed and waymarked path, which climbs the edge of pastures, dipping into and out of a narrow, dry valley before reaching the main A684. The main bus stops are 100 metres to the left, but if you are heading for Aysgarth Falls, café and toilets, cross straight ahead along the path by the parish church and steps by the old mill, to the Falls, continuing up the narrow path and steps behind to the main car park, cafe and National Park Centre.

Crummackdale
and Ingleborough
SETTLE TO INGLETON

FACT FILE

Distance: 15 miles (24 kilometres).

Maps: Harvey Dales West or OS Explorer OL30, OL41.

Terrain: An initial sharp climb over high pastures out of Ribblesdale between Stackhouses and Feizor is followed by delightful walking along narrow, enclosed packhorse tracks, before climbing steadily out of Crummackdale, along a section of the Three Peaks Walk with a steep ascent to Ingleborough summit and the long, stony track down to Ingleton.

Refreshment and accommodation: A good range of pubs and cafes in Settle and Ingleton but nothing else along the route, unless a half -mile diversion is made into Austwick (Game Cock Inn). Youth Hostel at Ingleton.

Toilets: Settle, Ingleton.

Transport: Outward: Regular train services on the Leeds-Settle-Carlisle line to Settle for the start of the walk, plus an hourly weekday bus from Skipton – Pennine Motors 580 (two-hourly on Saturdays) and 807 Dalesbus on summer Sundays. Return: Service 581 provides infrequent but conveniently timed journeys late afternoon and early evening back to Settle from Ingleton (bus stop outside Community Centre – site of old station); also service 80 to Lancaster. On Saturdays there is currently no early evening service, but the last Lancaster service (80) to High Bentham provides a good connection at Bentham station for trains to Giggleswick (for Settle), Skipton and Leeds. There are currently no Sunday bus services from Ingleton, but there is an evening train at Bentham – 3.5 miles (6km) by track and lane.

Stage point: Austwick or Clapham station (11 miles) – leave route at Wharfe; or Horton station (12 miles) – leave route at Sulber.

Drivers: Weekdays only: Park Ingleton and catch the morning 581 bus service to Settle.

Crummackdale is one of the smallest and least known of the Yorkshire dales, nestling in the shallow hollow between Ingleborough and Moughton Scar, a cul-de-sac valley without a through road except spectacular trails for the more intrepid walkers, cyclists and horse riders, and now including a section of the new Pennine Bridleway.

This is fairly strenuous walk, through some quintessential limestone country, dominated in its later stages by perhaps the most impressive of many routes up Yorkshire's most famous mountain and rewarded by some glorious views throughout.

Route

From Settle make your way along the main road or the quieter back ginnel (alleyway), which runs between houses just above Victoria Hall, to the bridge over the river. Take the Ribble Way path on the right around the school playing fields along the riverside to where it joins the Stackhouse road. Cross, the footpath going parallel to the road towards Stackhouse, where you take the path behind the hamlet, to the left, climbing uphill. At a signpost, turn sharp left, towards Feizor, the path climbing steeply uphill to a stile in the wall above. Keep the same direction, to the next stile, but now bearing slightly left. As you climb you are rewarded by fine views across the valley, with a notable and unusual view of Pen y Ghent across a section of limestone pavement known as Reinsber Scar.

Take the path along a rough vehicular track that bears left then right, still climbing, heading

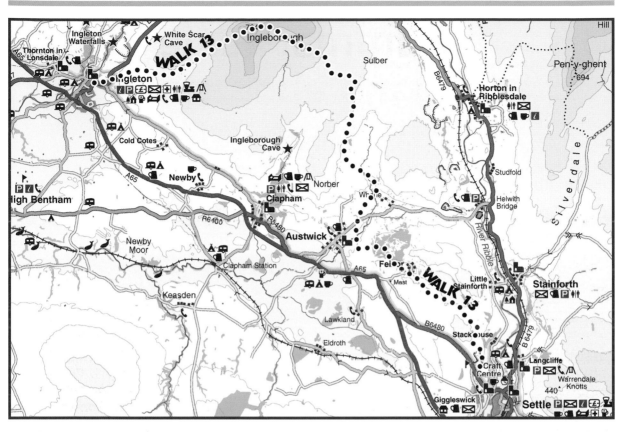

Storm-filled beck above Sulber Nick.

above the wall corner ahead, beyond which is a gate. The gradient levels, the path now following a wall, through gates over rough pasture. Take care at the end of the long pasture to go through the gate on the right to the other side of the wall, then the gate ahead. From here is a clear, well-marked path past scattered woodland known as Feizor Thwaite and down to the hamlet of Feizor, with your eventual destination, the summit of Ingleborough, an increasingly dominant feature ahead.

Feizor was once a staging post on an important trans-Pennine packhorse way, which according to some authorities linked Lancaster and York, crossing the Ribble at Stainforth packhorse bridge. Turn left into the hamlet but then turn first right along a concreted farm access track, which soon narrows to an ancient packhorse way, Hale Lane. Beyond Meldings Barn bear right and continue northwards to a junction of enclosed ways. Unless you are going to Austwick to the west, turn right along Wood Lane towards Wood End, turning right and left in the Helwith Bridge lane to another pretty hamlet, Wharfe, notable for a cottage with a large early Tudor chimney.

Immediately to the right the track to Crummackdale begins – a beautiful, winding wildflower-lined track that climbs below the edge of White Stone Scar and continues along the narrow enclosed valley. The track eventually descends to reach Wash Dub, an informal picnic area with a bench, little waterfall and slab footbridge, a point where the stream has created natural pool that until recently was used for sheep dipping. It is a delightful place to pause.

Keep along the lane until it meets the main farm road up Crummackdale, continuing to Crummack Farm, which fills the head of the dale. Follow the main track to the left of the

(Left) Bluebells along the narrow way above the hamlet of Wharfe.

farm, but rather than take the main bridleway to the left, signed Ingleborough, take the narrow footpath through the gate ahead. It crosses open pasture, marked by posts, heading for the great amphitheatre of crags that form the dale head. The path, well waymarked, climbs between these limestone outcrops. Look for the ladder stile and yellow waymarks. This is Beggar's Stile and it leads onto the great boggy expanse of equally evocatively named Thieves Moss. Keep on the path, which winds round to the left, around the top of the amphitheatre and up to a gate to link with the main bridlepath – known as Sulber Gate – from Crummackdale. Through the gate the path leads onto a high, bleak plateau. This is Sulber.

Keep ahead to the tall guideposts. Here you join the usually very busy track, much of its artificially engineered on sadly essential stone paving, steps, boardwalks or compacted quarry bottoms, which carries the Three Peaks Walk from Horton through Sulber Nick to Ingleborough. Millennia before its modern popularity, this was the ancient way, used by our Iron Age forefathers, from Ribblesdale to Ingleborough summit where there was a remarkable hill settlement or religious sanctuary.

At least path finding is straightforward from here. Turn left, the path climbing above and between impressive pavements, small streams and onto open moorland. Keep ahead; unless it is under cloud (which it frequently is), the summit of Ingleborough is the most impressive of all Dales landmarks and viewpoints. The path gradually ascends the shoulder of the hill until the summit ridge comes into view. It then becomes extremely steep over the last couple of hundred metres, more staircase than path, before the relief of the curiously level summit plateau.

Ingleborough has a long history as a beacon, one of the great chain of beacons across the north that in 1588 announced the arrival of the ill-fated Spanish Armada. For many years it was considered to be England's highest mountain, dominating as it does the horizon from

A characteristic view of Ingleborough from the west.

the Aire Gap and the Forest of Bowland to the Lancashire coast. In fact its 723 metres (2,373ft) is modest even by English standards, and is overshadowed by its far less prominent neighbour, Whernside, at 736 metres (2,419ft).

The latest archaeological research suggests that Ingleborough may have been an important Bronze or even Late Stone Age site used for religious or other rituals. Foundations of ring cairns are still clearly visible on the summit, though sadly the massive embankments have long been plundered for their stone, including the many walkers' cairns which dot the summit. Please do not desecrate this nationally important monument by attempting to move stone or build cairns, which could destroy vital evidence about the earliest inhabitants of the Dales.

In clear weather it is a magnificent viewpoint, providing a breathtaking panorama that makes every step of the climb worthwhile. On wild, wet, cloudy or misty days, when visibility may be a matter of three of four metres, the summit cairn and windbreaks offer at least a modicum of essential protection.

The route down is due south-west, stony and steeply stepped at first and requiring some care, but it soon becomes a broad, well-trodden track with good views all around. It descends past Crina Bottom Farm (fine view back to Ingleborough from here) and on to the outskirts of Ingleton. Turn left at the end of the track for some 400 metres to the top of the High Street, bearing right by the 'No Entry' signs into the village centre, with its tempting cafes, pubs and shops.

Ingleton, like other Dales villages, was once a mining centre, not this time lead but coal mining, situated as it is on once abundant coal measures. All signs of this industry – and indeed most of the more recent quarry industry – have long vanished, as has the Clapham – Tebay railway whose gaunt viaduct, mournful and disused, dominates the twin valleys of the Twiss and the Doe. But it is Ingleton's unforgettable waterfalls along the two rivers, which, like Ingleborough itself, have been drawing visitors here for well over a century.

WALK 14
The Whernside Ridge
INGLETON TO DENTDALE

Whernside is the highest but in some ways the least explored of Yorkshire's Three Peaks, away from the familiar Three Peaks Challenge Walk. This route links the popular village of Ingleton and its waterfalls with the magnificent ridge walk along the full length of the mountain, taking in its remote and mysterious tarns, and the ancient Craven Way into Dentdale.

Route

From Ingleton village centre head along the Thornton-in-Lonsdale road to the Waterfalls Walk entrance. There is a relatively high charge for entrance to this estate (no public right of way), but this section of route along the River Twiss past the magnificent falls, especially Pecca Falls and Thornton Force, is a highlight of the day and avoids a long road walk. Cash collected is used to maintain the many bridges and pathways in a safe condition.

Beyond Ravenray Bridge, the well peopled Waterfalls Walk joins and turns right into the Public Byway towards Beezley Falls, but before reaching the gate leading to Twistleton Hall Farm, take the bridleway left, marked by two wooden posts. This ascends at an acute angle, soon zigzagging back then bearing at right angles up the hillside towards limestone pavement. There are splendid views of Ingleborough, soon dominating the landscape to the east, and the great massif of Gragareth to the west. This track is Kirkby Gate, an ancient packhorse way which once led from Lancaster to Kirkby Stephen via Ingleton. Follow it through and past more limestone pavement and sink holes for about half a mile (or a kilometre) to a group of limestone boulders or erratics known as Standing Stones. Where one lies close to the path (and before reaching more limestone pavement), look for a narrow and faint path that curves off to the left and loops around, over higher and better

Thornton Force, where visitors can stand behind a curtain of water.

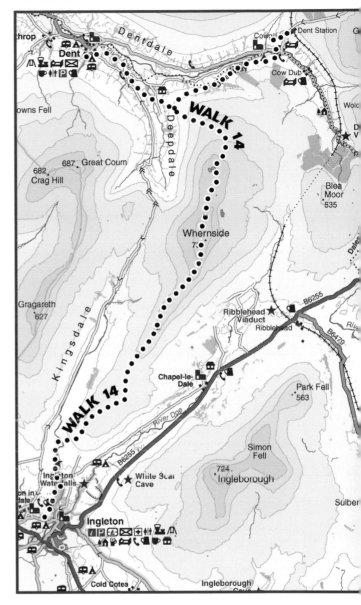

drained land, towards the long wall on the left.

At the wall is a faint path, which now climbs, gradually and steadily, along the ridge, with increasingly impressive views from either side, towards Rigg End and West Fell. This is a long but steady climb, over two miles (3km), with the path gradually getting clearer and better defined as you gain height. You cross a shallow dip or col, before heading towards the long summit ridge ahead. Eventually (and usually unmistakably in terms of large number of walkers met once again), you reach the two-metre wide Three Peaks Walk on the final, acute summit ascent. (Return path to Ribblehead from this point).

This is one of the great viewpoints of the Dales, 736 metres above sea level and the highest point in the Yorkshire Dales National Park. If you are lucky enough to get clear weather, the views extend across to Morecambe Bay and Heysham Power Station, as well as along the coast to Arnside Knott and the Kent estuary. The backcloth includes the peaks of the Lake District, the Howgills, Aye Gill Pike and Wild Boar Fell. There are equally splendid views down Ribblesdale itself, the mighty Ribblehead Viaduct looking like part of a child's toy railway as it snakes through the vast, bare landscape below.

Continue northwards, generally against the anticlockwise flow of Three Peaks' walkers,

(Above) An unusual view of Greensett Moss Tarn, an amazing 'flow-country' feature.
(Lower) A railway in a landscape –
Ribblehead Viaduct from Whernside summit.

looking down to Greensett Moss and its strange-shaped tarn below.

Where the Three Peaks paved route turns to descend sharp right, your way is the narrow, boggy path alongside a ruined wall on the left. After 250 metres a stile leads onto the open expanse of Knoutberry Hill. Keep the same direction, due north, along a faint but just discernible path bearing slightly left along Millstone Brow, a narrow headland with the Whernside tarns just to your left. It is worth strolling across the heather to enjoy their grand, even austere mountain setting. Otherwise keep to the path in the same direction, soon descending the brow of the hill. Keep to the right of the stone enclosure walls ahead to meet the Craven Way, the ancient bridle road between Ribblesdale and Dent, as it crosses the saddle of the fells.

This is a beautiful, broad green way, an old drovers' road, which curves down the fellside above Deepdale and towards the main valley of Dentdale. From here Dentdale almost looks like the side valley to the smaller Deepdale. Follow the track as it curves steeply downhill to a ladder stile, signed Laithbank. There are magnificent views into fertile, green Dentdale from here, its scattering of small fields, woods, barns and hedgerows a rich contrast to the bleakness of Ribblesdale. The village of Dent with its distinctive church, is in the middle distance, with Combe Scar, Helms Knott and the Howgills beyond.

If you are heading for Dent village (21 km) your route is along the Craven Way into the main valley close to where Deepdale meets Dentdale. You pick up the line of the Dales Way along Deepdale Beck beyond Mill Bridge, and then follow the banks of the Dee to

Along the Craven Way.

Church Bridge and along the lane to Dent with its welcoming inns and cafes.

However, for Dent station cross the stile to Laithbank. This path contours the hillside through tall moor grass – posts mark the way – eventually crossing stiles and a couple of small fields to meet a lower path to Laithbank. Keep right through stiles behind Laithbank Farm to join the Dales Way – look for the stile on the right of the farm drive. From here it is a matter of following the (fairly) well waymarked Dales Way path as it goes via West Clint, Coat Faw, Hackergill and Little Town plantation to Ewegales, then the riverside to Lea Yeat. Allow a good half hour for the murderously steep ascent up the lane to Dent station for your train.

Wild Boar Fell

GARSDALE TO KIRKBY STEPHEN

This ramble from the Settle-Carlisle line, between Garsdale and Kirkby Stephen, is perhaps the most spectacular of all from the celebrated railway, a favourite of Dales Rail walkers from the 1970s onwards. It follows a massive, extended mountain ridge over three linked peaks – Swarth Fell, Wild Boar Fell and Little Fell – which gives glorious views throughout. Not to be attempted by the unfit or faint hearted, nor in low cloud or mist, as there is no shelter or facilities over thirteen miles of wild and rugged terrain. But fell walking, anywhere in the UK, doesn't get much better than this.

Route

From Garsdale station follow the drive and lane down to the main road. Almost opposite the junction is a gap stile and sign marked to Grisedale and Flust. Take the path as it ascends the rush-filled hillside, keeping the stone wall about 20 metres to your left to locate a stile, 10 metres east of a gate ahead. The path, now marked by stiles and finger posts, continues in roughly the same direction, following a narrow gill and then heading above a stone barn before dropping into Grisedale. Head for the white farmhouse flanked by two stone barns ahead, past another derelict barn, emerging on a tarmac farm road to the left of the farmhouse. Turn right along the lane, climbing up to and beyond East House cottage.

Follow what soon becomes a stone track as it curves to the right. Around 100 metres from the bend, the public bridleway, not easily visible on the ground, heads at right angles up the hillside with Turner Hill to your left. Keep on higher bits of ground away from boggy areas as you climb, with luck locating the faint path, heading for the post and wire fence ahead where you will almost certainly see the twin-lane grassy path. Turn left to follow the fence, keeping it on your left as you head towards Swarth Fell, the first peak ahead. Keep on the grass path as you leave the wire fence, dipping down to go alongside another section

FACT FILE

Distance: To Kirkby Stephen station 13 miles (21 kilometres); to Kirkby Stephen town 14 miles (23 kilometres).

Maps: Harvey Dales West; OS Explorer OL19.

Terrain: Mainly open moorland, rough fell country, boggy in places, plus some tracks at the end of the walk. A strenuous walk, with three major ascents – and a climb to the station.

Refreshment and accommodation: Inns, B&Bs, cafes and shops in Kirkby Stephen. No other facilities anywhere along the route, so take adequate supplies of food and water.

Toilets: Garsdale station or Kirkby Stephen town (NB: No facilities at Kirkby Stephen station).

Transport: Outward and Return: Well timed services for this walk operate daily to Garsdale and Kirkby Stephen along the Leeds-Settle-Carlisle line.

Staging Point: None. If poor weather prevails, return from Turner Hill – 3 miles.

Drivers: Park Garsdale station and return from Kirkby Stephen – or leave the car at Skipton or Settle to enjoy the unforgettable journey over the summit of the Settle-Carlisle line.

of fence to where you meet a crossing fence. Locate a wooden step stile in the corner where the two fences meet (this is all now Public Access land).

Your way now follows the clear path on the right-hand side of the next fence, along what is the longest and toughest haul of the day. There are stretches of bog to navigate around (the path avoids most but not all of these), compensated by ever more dramatic views of the Howgill Fells to the west. You eventually head up and reach the cairn on Swarth Fell Pike (651 metres) with fine views of the Eden Valley to the north and east.

Keep on the ridge, dipping down past a small tarn and climbing to the next summit cairn, the highest point on Swarth Fell (681 metres), with a fine view over to Wild Boar Fell itself opening out. The way is clear to see ahead, alongside the wall, dipping down the great saddle between Swarth and Wild Boar Fell, past a second, larger tarn. Continue to follow the wall and fence for a couple of hundred metres past the tarn, to where a narrow but very clear path bears off diagonally to the right, up the slope ahead known as The Band, and climbs to the great flat summit plateau of Wild Boar Fell itself.

The summit trig point (708 metres) is actually to your left, but the main path heads for the edge of the fell with its breathtaking views into the Mallerstang valley, curving round the sharp nose of the hill. A line of tall cairns and a stile indicate The Nab. This a wonderful viewpoint, with Mallerstang Edge across the valley opposite and, if the weather is clear, panoramas all around which include the North Pennines, the Stainmore Gap, the Lakeland Fells and even, on the clearest days, the peak of Criffell in Scotland across the Solway Firth.

Wild Boar Fell owes it name to being reputedly the place where the last native wild boar in England was shot in the seventeenth century. The late Tom Stephenson, first secretary of the Ramblers' Association, one of the founding fathers of the National Park movement and creator of the Pennine Way, once

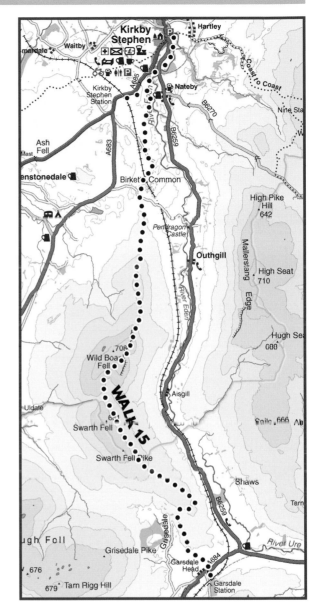

confessed that Wild Boar Fell was his favourite hill in all England. Once you have climbed this most distinctive of Dales hills you will understand why. If current plans are realised, Wild Boar Fell, Mallerstang and the northern Howgills may soon be incorporated in the Yorkshire Dales National Park, which will safeguard them from being tamed and urbanised into gigantic 'wind farms'.

The descent from The Nab is to head for Little Fell directly ahead, across another saddle, ignoring crossing paths (the Pennine

Bridleway) and keeping to the right of the wall up Little Fell. At 559 metres the name 'Little' is purely relative, with a surprisingly steep climb to the summit. This time the views are down into the fertile, green valley of the Upper Eden, the spires and rooftops of Kirkby Stephen in the middle distance ahead.

Your way down is along the grassy path ahead to the left of a large enclosure surrounding an area of heather. Keep to the left of this wall, but at an angle in the wall take the faint path which branches off left, almost due north past swallow holes. It soon joins a faint green way, which becomes an elevated grass road, perhaps an old peat cutters' track, across Greenlaw Rigg.

You eventually reach and cross Tommy Road, a tarmac lane from Pendragon, keeping in the same direction to pick up and follow the broad green track ahead. Follow this to the bridge over the railway at Greengate and down to the lane south of Bull Gill. Opposite Bull Gill is an enclosed, green bridleway, a little overgrown with nettles in the summer months,

Green Gates – an old drovers' way near Lammerside.

which goes along the edge of field, eventually leading into open pasture. Keep along the wall side through gates and a stile to Wharton Hall.

Follow the concrete farm road from Wharton for 800 metres to the cottage at Halfpenny House. The railway station lies over the stile left, alongside the wall up three fields to steps leading into the station drive. For Kirkby Stephen town, the pleasantest way is to turn right, through gates (signed Skenrith and waymarked) and across a field to a stile, leading to a pretty riverside path. Go round the edge of a wood to the riverside at Skenrith, with steps and railings alongside a rocky gorge of the Eden, and on to Skenrith Bridge. At the road turn left for 20 metres, then take the path to the right and back along the riverside below Skenrith Hill to a footbridge. Turn right over the river and left at the junction to join the pleasant riverside path, crossing Frank's Bridge

to head into the centre of Kirkby Stephen.

If it is quick refreshment in Kirkby Stephen you are seeking, a walk straight down the drive from Halfpenny House takes you directly into the town, but it is a good kilometre (half a mile) along a busy main road into the town centre. Allow at least 45 minutes to walk back to

Stenkrith gorge, on the path into Kirkby Stephen town.

Halfpenny House and up to the station, as it is uphill all the way and trains are not to be missed.

WALK 16

Lady Anne's Way

HAWES (GARSDALE) - KIRKBY STEPHEN

This walk links the wild country at the head of Wensleydale with the beautiful Eden Valley in Cumbria. Much of the route follows the prehistoric High Way, an ancient ridge-way that was in constant use from Bronze Age times as a trade route and packhorse way until the eighteenth century turnpike road was built in the valley. Its most famous regular traveller was the redoubtable Lady Anne Clifford of Skipton and Appleby, Countess of Pembroke, who frequently travelled with her carriage and retainers over the ancient road that linked her many properties. First popularised as one of the Dales Rail walks in the late 1970s, a 100-mile long-distance trail, Lady Anne's Way, has been developed between Skipton and Penrith, using the High Way and other paths. The High Way is also being improved to form part of the Pennine Bridleway. Incorporating some fine link paths via Cotterdale from Hawes, this walk makes a magnificent route across the watershed between the two valleys, which can be shortened by starting or finishing at Garsdale station on the Settle-Carlisle line.

FACT FILE

Distance: 19 miles (30 kilometres); to Garsdale station 11.5 miles (18km); from Garsdale station to Kirkby Stephen 13 miles (21km).

Maps: Harvey Dales North; OS Explorer OL19.

Terrain: Field paths and tracks, with some rough, boggy areas on the Garsdale link. Two significant ascents, the first moderate, the second steep.

Refreshment and accommodation: Green Dragon, Inn, Hardraw; Moorcock Inn, Garsdale (1 mile from station on A684); Black Bull Inn and shop, Nateby. Several pubs and cafes in Kirkby Stephen. Youth Hostel: Hawes. Choice of B&Bs in Hawes and Kirkby Stephen.

Toilets: Hawes, Garsdale station, Kirkby Stephen town (nothing at station).

Transport: Outward: Weekdays: Morning trains Leeds-Skipton-Settle-Garsdale for 113 bus to Hawes; 156, 157 Northallerton-Hawes. Sundays: 800, 805 Leeds-Ilkley-Hawes, 807; Skipton-Settle-Hawes. Return: Late afternoon and early evening trains from Kirkby Stephen to Garsdale, Settle, Skipton and Leeds.

Stage point: Garsdale station - see above.

Drivers: Park Garsdale, catch bus to Hawes, return on train from Kirkby Stephen; alternatively stage the walk to/from Garsdale.

Route

From Hawes follow the Pennine Way north along the Thwaite road, soon cutting across the corner along the flagged path and rejoining the road to cross the river. After 150 metres take the Pennine Way through the meadows and over stiles to Hardraw, where it is worth taking a little time to visit the famous Hardraw Force reached through the Green Dragon inn.

Continue along the Pennine Way, which takes an enclosed stony track some 40 metres west of the inn, gradually climbing up and beyond a small wood, getting steeper as it ascends Bluebell Hill, to reach a gate and wall where the track divides. Keep to the left fork, the Pennine Way, but as the track curves in a zigzag some 120 metres above the gate, take the narrow path left, signed Cotterdale. This is a beautiful route across rough, sloping moor

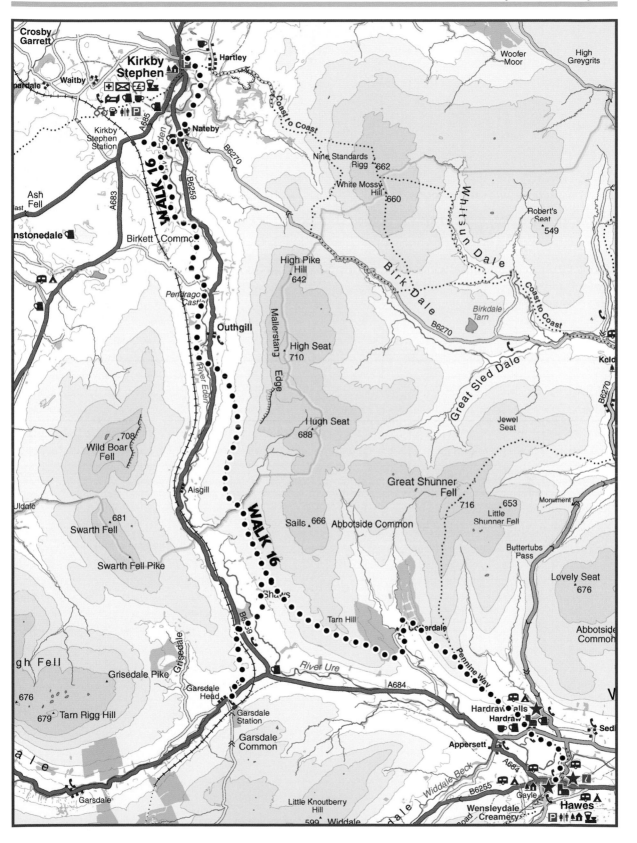

grass, with an ever more impressive unfolding panorama of the high fells opposite. Widdale, Ten End, Wether Fell, Addlebrough and finally Pen Hill dominate the view of the valley as it spreads out behind you. Ahead is the sharp summit of Cotter End – soon to be tackled.

The path, faint through the grass but marked by stiles and the occasional signpost or waymark, gradually turns into the little hidden valley of Cotterdale. Pass a sheepfold and descend slightly towards and below a line of old quarry workings, the path almost obliterated by bracken. The path goes through a stile to the right of a small barn, alongside a wall, before eventually going through the wall and across a field to the wall below. At a junction of paths, take the more obvious way left over a little footbridge, crossing the next fields (follow waymarks and stiles) eventually to reach the riverside. Turn right along Cotterdale Beck. Before reaching the hamlet of Cotterdale, cross the concrete bridge to return along the far side of the beck. Cross the field to a hump-backed footbridge over a side beck, then alongside the stream to the wall corner and along the next

field, before finally turning up the field side to where a stile leads to the Cotterdale lane.

Cross the path (signed to Thwaite Bridge), slightly to the right, which climbs steadily up rough pasture, the gradient suddenly increasing up the steep fellside to the wall and stile on the brow of the hill. Keep ahead to the next stile where you join the ancient green High Way – Lady Anne's Way – as it climbs Cotter Riggs, between a wire fence and stone wall. Lady Anne's diaries record her travelling this way over Cotter End and Hell Gill, although how her unsprung coach managed this murderous gradient is hard to imagine.

Your way is up the very steep track to the crest of Cotter End ahead. In clear weather there are fine glimpses of the surrounding fells with, intriguingly, the summit of Ingleborough just visible as you climb. A welcome bench almost at the top gives a chance to catch your breath and enjoy superb views down Wensleydale as far as Pen Hill. Once on the top of the ridge you join

Old Barn, Cotterdale.

The old Highway climbing Cotter End.

a superb grassy way, almost level, which follows the great curve of the valley as its turns northwards, soon with views down to the viaduct over Dandry Mire and the course of the former Wensleydale railway below. Your route is along this wonderful old green way for around two miles (3km), with the magnificent outline and twin peaks of Swarth Fell and Wild Boar Fell soon visible, the latter's distinct craggy outline dominating the view.

You reach to a ruined building on the left. This is High Dyke which up to the early nineteenth century and the building of the turnpike road in the valley below, was a popular packhorse and drovers' inn, providing refreshment and overnight accommodation (with free grazing) in this wild location.

If you are curtailing the walk, there is a short cut down to Blades for Garsdale, but more attractive is to continue for another kilo-metre, a little over half a mile, to just past a beck, new footbridge and gate, where the line of fir trees meets the High Way. A stile leads to a field. Head to the wall ahead and follow it downhill and round to the left, keeping above the wall of Shaws, once a Youth Hostel, to find steep stone steps in the corner. Go through a gate and down past waterfalls to a footbridge. This leads to a path past a second footbridge and through a semi-deserted farmyard to the tiny chapel at Lunds, one of the most remote and evocative places in the higher Dales.

The path, waymarked to the west of Lunds, climbs a low hill beyond. Follow the line of stile and faint path over tussocky grass and rushes in the same direction, taking the stile to the left and the path alongside the wall. At the

Wild Boar Fell from near Lunds.

next wall and fence corner on the right, a stile leads to a path over increasingly tough rushes. Keep ahead to the white Blades footbridge over the infant River Ure. Take the little pedestrian gate left before heading up towards the barn ahead, to the right of which a stile leads up to South Lunds farm – the path is between the farm and the large agricultural building, marked by gates.

Cross the main B6255 and take the path almost opposite to the footbridge over the railway. Bear left at the railway along the faint path through rough moor grass that climbs the drumlin of Cock Lakes, ahead. Keep the same direction, almost due south, the path marked by stiles (look for the ladder stile slightly to the right) and eventually join the main A684 some 250 metres before the lane to Garsdale station. If you seek refreshment at the Moorcock before your train, it is a 15-minute walk along the A684.

For the full route to Kirkby Stephen (if joining from Garsdale use route above in reverse),

you will have remained on the High Way above Shaws. Keep ahead on this lovely green way – now part of the Pennine Bridleway and repaired in places as a stony track – to High Hall, another impressive ruined farm. Streams here form the headwaters of the River Ure, heading for the North Sea, but you cross the watershed of the Pennines a few metres ahead as you descend slightly to reach Hell Gill, a bridge across a deep chasm through which the infant River Eden roars on its way to the Solway Firth and Irish Sea.

The High Way now drifts gently across Hellgill Wold, with splendid views down and into the Eden Valley with Wild Boar Fell on your left and Mallerstang Edge on your right. It finally descends down the recently much improved and metalled track through rough pastures into Mallerstang, the name given to the upper Eden Valley. Follow the track down to the main B6259 road near Thrang.

Take the farm track almost opposite, which goes down to Thrang Bridge over the Eden, taking the riverside path sharp right. Continue to the next farm, then keep ahead by woodland and riverside to Shoregill. The path enters a pleasant area of riverside pasture across the next three fields, before finally, at a junction, heading through a narrow field to the riverside opposite Pendragon Castle. It is worth following the lane back over Castle Bridge to view the castle, according to local legend the birthplace of Celtic prince Uther Pendragon, father of King Arthur. In fact there is no evidence that there was a castle here before the present Norman structure, built in the twelfth century and restored in the seventeenth by Lady Anne Clifford (of course), who here broke her journeys northwards. The castle is on private land but access is permitted providing visitors respect the monument.

From Pendragon, follow the lane back uphill but at the next sharp bend take the track right which goes around a beautiful curve of the river below Birkett Common, a limestone outcrop that indicates the line of the Pennine Fault. North of here lies the typical red sandstone country of Cumbria. Where the track finally reaches Cropp House farm, a gate on the right gives access to the bridleway past the ruins of Lammerside Castle, another twelfth century structure, fortified into a pele tower in the fourteenth century as a defence against frequent Scottish Raids.

Keep ahead on the bridleway, the route marked by gates, until it joins the concrete farm road past Wharton Hall, another magnificent medieval fortified house, this time still a fully functional working farm. If you are heading for Kirkby Stephen town with its creature comforts, look for the footpath right, some 100 metres beyond Wharton Hall, which leads to the footbridge and paths to Nateby village, with its inn. Take the Reeth road (B6270) for 150 metres to where on the left a narrow way follows Broad Ing Sike behind the village. This becomes a beautiful enclosed packhorseway, which eventually crosses the old Stainmore railway. Keep slightly right at the fork to the woodland ahead, from where a riverside path leads to Frank's Bridge and the centre of Kirkby.

If you are heading for the train, keep to the main concrete farm road beyond Wharton Hall for 800 metres to Halfpenny House, almost opposite which a stile leads on the left to the new path alongside the edge of fields, following the wall by Whinny Hill directly up to Kirkby Stephen station.

Over Apedale

LEYBURN - REDMIRE - REETH

This is a classic dale to dale walk, linking central Wensleydale and Swaledale, a contrast of fertile woods and gentle pastures within the two dales, with a crossing of bleak moorland dividing the two. The moor is rich in relics of the great lead mining industry as well as older archaeological remains from Iron Age times onwards. It is also a delight for green travellers, offering a chance to combine the walk by making use

On Leyburn Shawl.

of local buses or the newly reopened Wensleydale Railway to Leyburn or Redmire, and the Swaledale bus service.

Route

From Leyburn market place follow the sign for Leyburn Shawl from the north-western corner of the square, past Commercial Square, along a cul-de-sac road leading to a pedestrian gate on the left. This is a popular afternoon walk from Leyburn, soon ascending a long, narrow ridge, above Shawl Wood, through gates and stiles. As you climb, there are ever

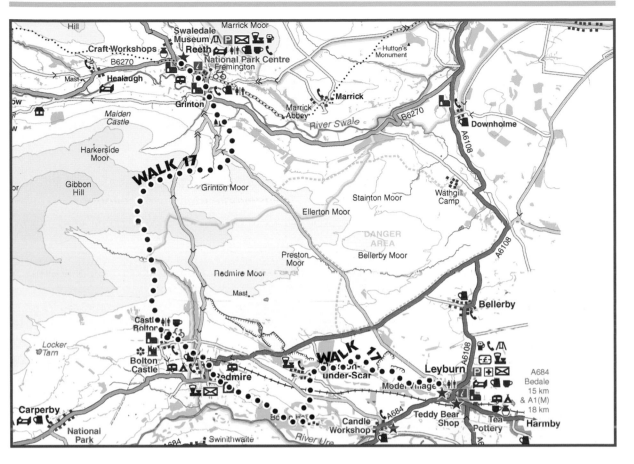

grander views across and along the whole length of mid-Wensleydale, with Pen Hill majestic in the foreground and Addlebrough just visible beyond.

Keep ahead along the summit of the ridge, maintaining the same direction past Warren Wood to locate a path, near the end of the wood, through stiles on the left. It swings down towards Gillfield Wood ahead. Follow the waymarks as the path twists thorough the wood, over a footbridge, eventually emerging in the lane some 200 metres east of Preston-under-Scar.

FACT FILE

Distance: 14 miles (22 kilometres).

Maps: Harvey Dales North; OS Explorer OL30.

Terrain: Woodland and moorland tracks, footpaths across pastureland, with some areas of open moorland. Two long but moderate climbs.

Refreshment and accommodation: Village inns at Redmire and Grinton. Café at Castle Bolton in Castle. Cafes and pubs in Reeth. Youth Hostel at Grinton Lodge (accessible near the end of the walk).

Toilets: Leyburn, Castle Bolton, Grinton and Reeth.

Transport: Outward: Service 159 from Richmond and Ripon; 156, 157 from Northallerton to Leyburn, 157 or Wensleydale Railway to Leyburn or Redmire. Return: Service 30, 30A from Reeth to Richmond (for Darlington). Summer Sundays: Dalesbus 802, 803, 807.

Stage point: Redmire (6.75 miles, 11km) – return to Leyburn by Wensleydale Railway or 157.

Drivers: Park Richmond, catch 159 to Leyburn, 30 back from Richmond (or Leyburn if doing the Redmire section only). On Fridays it is possible to park in Reeth and catch the morning market day bus (36) to Leyburn and walk back to a parked vehicle.

Grinton Mill and peat store, with flue in the background – one of the grandest surviving monuments of Dales lead mining.

Just beyond the cross roads in the village, look for the path, left, between houses, which soon curves to the left before descending to cross the Wensleydale Railway and the Redmire road at Stoneham Cottage. The route now follows the public right of way almost opposite, along the farm access road down to where it meets the track past Bolton Hall Farm, close to Bolton Hall, then turning right along the long track that climbs through West Wood. This becomes a field path marked by gates and stiles along pastures above the river, eventually joining Well Lane, a narrow tarmac track that leads into Redmire. Turn right into the village, but left at the first fork by the village green, heading towards Castle Bolton. This leads up to Redmire station, the present western terminus of the Wensleydale Railway.

Unless you are returning to Leyburn or Leeming by train, follow the footpath alongside the railway line. It crosses two becks before heading off, after around 300 metres, diagonally uphill directly towards Bolton Castle. This magnificent late fourteenth century castle, built by Richard Scrope, Lord Chancellor of England, is a major landmark. It once held Mary Queen of Scots as a prisoner. It is well worth combining visit to the castle with the walk. The village of Castle Bolton has a charming, extended village green along its length, and a fascinating mid fourteenth century church.

The track to Swaledale begins from the village green, about 50 metres east of the castle, as a stony, enclosed bridleway that winds up to open moorland. Keep the stone wall about 20 metres to your left and climb the moorland, eventually joining a more clearly defined track that swings to the right between wire fences and climbs Black Hill to a gate. This becomes a fine green way, descending into a shallow valley, Apedale, past a sheepfold and small farm buildings known as Dent's Houses at a junction of tracks. Follow the track directly ahead, climbing through heather and past grouse shooting butts to the Height of Greet at a cairn and old mine working.

From the crest of the hill, some 500 metres above sea level, there are magnificent views over the surrounding moors into Swaledale if the weather is clear. Continue on the main track as it descends and bears right after the summit, over a stream, eventually joining the Grinton to Redmire road at an informal parking area.

Straight opposite you will see a deep, almost dry valley. This is Ridley Hush. Hushing was a popular technique in lead mining, whereby a narrow stream close to or on a main lead vein was dammed. After sufficient water had built up behind it, the dam was released, the scouring action of the water and debris washing out chunks of galena or lead ore which could be hacked out of the stream bed.

This part of Grinton Moor is Common Land, enjoying new public access under the CROW Act. With care, follow a narrow path along the top right-hand edge of the hush, which descends to a spoil tip. Cross the beck below the tip to follow the edge of the moor and emerge at Grinton Smelt Mill.

This is perhaps the best-preserved relic of the lead mining industry in the whole of the Yorkshire Dales – a substantial building with a nearby peat fuel store. A long stone flue that ascends the hillside was designed to improve the draught in the furnace and remove toxic fumes of lead. This water-powered mill was built relatively late in the lead mining era and did not enjoy a long life of service. Interpretive boards in the mill explain the history and how it all worked.

Follow a narrow path to the left-hand side of the flue. About half way up, look for a path which branches off to the left, below the scar ahead. This bears left to merge with the bridleway as a grassy track, heading towards Cogden Hall, soon crossing the Leyburn to Reeth road. Keep ahead for another 300 metres. At a gate, follow the footpath (not visible on the ground), which bears at 45 degrees to the left, descending to a shallow stream behind Grinton Lodge Youth Hostel. Here a little gate and stile lead to a narrow path to the stream – to be forded with care.

The waymarked path now leads through fields with a choice of ways into Grinton village, with its welcoming Bridge Inn. It is worth spending a little time to admire the twelfth century Grinton church, before crossing Grinton Bridge and taking the field path past Fremington to emerge at Reeth Bridge.

Once a focal point for the lead mining trade, and now a popular centre for visitors, there are few pleasanter places to end a walk and wait for a bus than Reeth, with its spectacular views, handsome village green, shops, pubs and cafes. You might even be tempted to stay a little longer in the area with a good choice of overnight accommodation including the splendidly refurbished Youth Hostel at Grinton.

The Wensleydale Walk
HAWES - ASKRIGG - REDMIRE

Wensleydale offers some magnificent linear walks, especially if you choose some of the *higher-level routes along the shoulders of the valley. This walk takes advantage of several such routes along the central part of the dale, as well as good public transport links between the villages, to give a choice of opportunities to explore this fine, open dale.*

FACT FILE

Distance: 14 miles (22 kilometres).

Maps: Harvey Dales East; OS Explorer OL30.

Terrain: Mainly farm tracks, quiet lanes and field paths across pasture. Some steep sections, but generally moderate.

Refreshment and accommodation: Wide choice of inns, Youth Hostel, cafes, B&Bs in Hawes; pubs, shops, café, B&B in Askrigg; café and pub in Bainbridge (1.5 miles from Askrigg); pub in Warton (1 mile from Askrigg); café at Castle Bolton (in castle); pub and B&B in Redmire.

Toilets: Hawes, Bainbridge, Castle Bolton.

Transport: Outward: Hawes can be accessed by Dales & District 156 and 157 bus services from Northallerton (connection at Northallerton station) and Leyburn, and by service 113 from Garsdale station on the Settle Carlisle line (weekdays), or Dales Bus services 800, 805 and 807 on summer Sundays and Bank Holidays (805 Sundays all year). Return: Bus 157 approximately every two to three hours, daily from Redmire to Hawes, via Askrigg, or to Leyburn and Northallerton. Wensleydale Railway train service operates from Redmire station to Leyburn or Leeming Bar (bus link to Northallerton) – on days of operation (08454 505474) approximately every two hours. The walk can also be shortened by taking field paths from above Kendalacre to Carperby for Aysgarth Falls corner for 156 or 800, 805, 807.

Stage point: Askrigg (6.5 miles, 10km) for 157 bus, or walk to Worton (1 mile, 1.3km) for 156 or Dalesbus 800, 805, 807.

Drivers: Park Hawes and return on 157 from Redmire to Hawes.

Route

From Hawes Countryside Centre and bus terminus, take the Askrigg road northwards, following the paved Pennine Way path to cut the corner to Haylands Bridge and then taking the first path on the right. This crosses to a little footbridge before ascending a wide field to the main Askrigg road. Cross and take the path almost opposite, climbing sharply to the left up to Sedbusk.

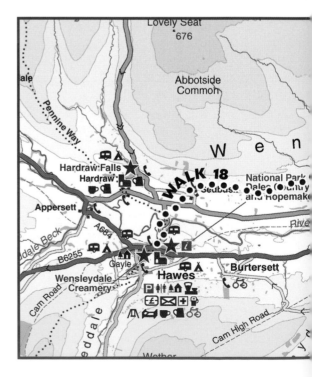

Turn right in the village, along the lane heading to the road junction before picking up the path from the eastern end of Sedbusk, par-

Askrigg village from the east.

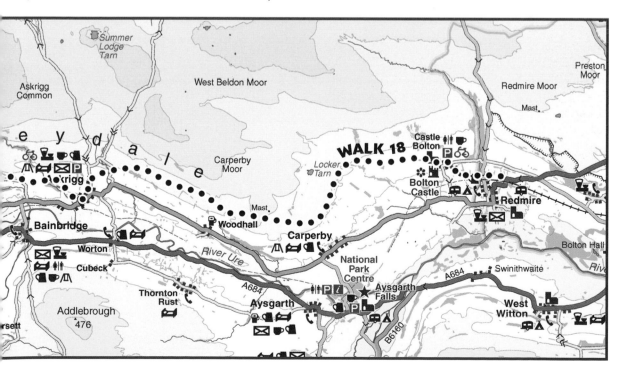

allel to but above the lane, marked by a series of stiles across the pastures to the hamlet of Litherskew. There are fine views back across the dale to Hawes and Wether Fell. The path continues through more stiles in the same direction, eventually joining a green track above enclosure walls and old quarry workings. This track now parallels the hillside, past Shaw Cote farm, before gradually climbing up to Skell Gill and meeting Skell Gill Lane.

Follow the lane to the junction below Helm, turning sharply downhill, but after 120 metres, where the lane bends to the right, take the gateway on the left along a track above the wall which heads towards Mill Gill. Just beyond the junction of paths where the track ends, look for a little pedestrian gate in the wall

Ox Close Road – a high level green way that follows the contours above Wensleydale's valley floor.

ahead that leads into the wood above Mill Gill Force. Follow the path for a couple of hundred metres down to one of the prettiest, if almost hidden, waterfalls in Wensleydale.

Return to the pedestrian gate but now follow the path to the left along the top of the gill. Stay inside the enclosed woodland along the wall on the edge of the gill, eventually emerging behind the buildings of the old mill that gave the valley its name. Turn left and then bear right to join the flagged path that emerges at the west end of Askrigg village.

Askrigg achieved literary and television fame as the fictional village of Darrowby in the James Herriot's nostalgic novels of a Dales veterinary practice in the immediate post war years. The King's Arms Inn, aka The Drovers, became almost like a revered film set. Fiction apart, Askrigg is an interesting linear village, with a fine parish church and market cross (its market charter was granted in 1587) and was once famous for its clock makers. Some 100 metres above

Bolton Castle, where Mary Queen of Scots was once imprisoned.

the King's Head, with its fine sign, broad stones steps on the right lead into a typical Yorkshire alleyway or ginnel between cottages.

Turn left at the junction to take a pretty path behind houses and gardens, soon leaving the village to cross small fields up Stony Bank, through stiles, towards the hamlet of Newbiggin. Cross the lane into an estate road through new housing to pick up the path to the right, behind the bungalows, which leads through a little gate. Take the higher of the two paths, which climbs to the left. Keep the same direction, climbing steeply across more small fields towards the farm buildings and wood. Your route is to the right, through the gate into and diagonally up through the wood eventually to join a fine green lane at Heugh. Turn right here, the reward for the climbing being a beautiful level track with magnificent views along the dale, with Addlebrough almost opposite but Penhill increasingly dominant.

The track now follows a low ridge. Continue for the next mile (1.6km) to where,

above Woodhall, you need to go through the gate on the left to join the continuation of the route along another track, this time known as Oxclose Road. This is a beautiful, distinctive green way, curving below Ivy Scar with its extensive, amazingly exposed old lead mine workings, gently climbing above New Pasture. Crossing tracks lead down to Carperby for anyone who needs return transport from this village or Aysgarth. Otherwise the grassy way curves northwards – keep to the less obvious path straight ahead at a fork by Oxclose Gate to cross a series of long fields. You meet the popular circular walk from Bolton Castle, which is soon in view as you head north. The track fords a shallow beck as it turns eastwards – the castle now surprisingly invisible behind trees as you get closer.

Above the woodland that shelters Beldon

Mill Gill Falls, Askrigg – a silvery column of water hidden in a thickly wooded gill.

down towards Castle Bolton. The magnificent fourteenth century castle and museum are well worth a visit, as is the little thirteenth century village church of St Oswald. Should you wish to spend more time here, the 157 bus for Hawes, Northallerton or Leyburn also serves the village.

For the walk into Redmire, head for the far end of the village. Here a track on the right (signed) heads to a gate and stile, 80 metres below which a stile, left, gives access to a path that crosses the fields diagonally down to the railway track. If you are heading to Redmire station, the present terminus of the Wensleydale Railway, turn left alongside the trackbed, soon crossing a stream at a footbridge to emerge in the lane by the station entrance.

For Redmire itself continue over the railway track, the path turning left along the field edge and crossing Apedale Beck into the village. There is a shop and inn if there is time to fill before your bus.

If you are tempted to continue the walk to Leyburn – 6.5 miles or 10 kilometres – there is a lovely route via Well Lane, West Wood, Bolton Park, Preston-under-Scar, Warren Wood and Leyburn Shawl (see Walk 17)

Beck, take care to go through a gate on your right to follow the wall above the gill, going through the next gate to keep the wall on your right. The path becomes a good farm track, passing sheepfolds before curving to the right

WALK 19
Upper Swaledale
KELD TO REETH

Upper Swaledale contains some of the most hauntingly beautiful countryside of the Yorkshire Dales. Kisdon hill and the narrow gorge of the upper Swale dominate the start of this spectacular walk, which, below Muker, follows the river through some typical herb-rich ancient meadows to the old Viking and later lead mining settlement of Gunnerside. Below Gunnerside the route goes along the hillside through Rowleth Wood before crossing the river to reach Low Lane, a deep sunken track leading to riverside paths and the little suspension bridge below Reeth. Please walk in single file through the many meadows passed on this walk to minimise damage to this important crop.

Route

From the bus stop on the main road in Keld walk down to the centre of the hamlet, taking the path that starts at a gate in the bottom right-hand corner. Keep ahead at the first junction of paths.

After some 200 metres beyond this junction, a narrow path signed Upper Falls is reached on the left. This is an extraordinarily beautiful path, but steep and only suitable for the agile – with the occasional fallen tree. It leads down the steep hillside to cliffs above the Upper and Middle Falls, a magnificent viewpoint, dominated by woods, waterfalls and limestone scars, but requiring the greatest care. Unless you are scrambling down to the falls, the path (not a right of way) continues along and up the hillside to rejoin the main path. If you are nervous or not especially agile, and

choose to stay on the main path, keep left at the junction with the Pennine Way some 100 metres further along, soon rejoining the narrow path from the Falls.

This is now a particularly lovely way along Kisdon Side, with fine views across the valley towards Crackpot Hall and Swinner Gill, with the remains of lead mining visible along the hillside opposite. At one point the path is a narrow,

FACT FILE

Distance: 12 miles (19 kilometres).

Maps: Harvey Dales North or OS Explorer OL30.

Terrain: A mixture of stony tracks, pasture and meadowland. No steep ascents, with fairly easy walking throughout.

Refreshment and accommodation: Café in Keld; Farmers Arms and café in Muker; King's Head Inn and café in Gunnerside; choice of cafes and pubs in Reeth. Youth Hostel in Grinton (2 miles south of Reeth), B&B in Reeth.

Toilets: Keld, Muker, Gunnerside, Reeth

Transport: Outward: Weekdays: Dales Bus 30, the Swaledale Bus, from Richmond to Keld (connections from Darlington). Sundays: Summer only 830 direct from Darlington and Richmond to Thwaite. Alight Thwaite – then two miles by field path and lane to Keld.

Return: Weekdays bus 30 to Richmond late afternoon and early evening; 830 on Sundays.

Stage point: Muker (3 miles) by meadow path from footbridge into village; Gunnerside 6.5 miles then service 30/830 into Reeth or Richmond.

Drivers: Park Reeth to catch outward service 30/830 from the Green, walking back to vehicle.

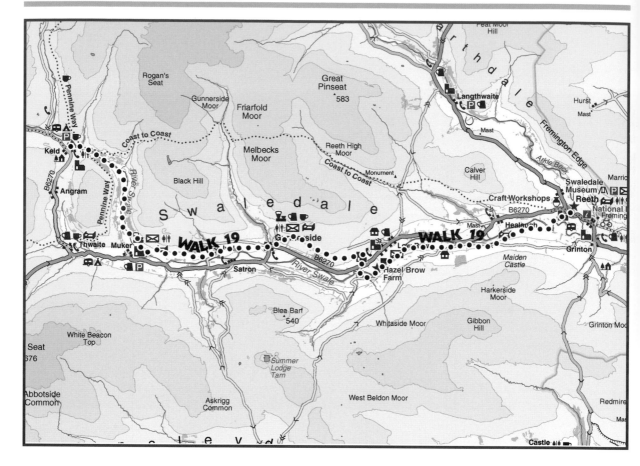

ancient way enclosed by trees, passing old barns, gradually descending the hillside to go through meadows. At a junction of paths, take the path left, marked by gated stiles, which eventually crosses to the riverside and the footbridge.

If you wish to visit the delightful village of Muker, take the stile on the right before the bridge approach, which leads to a path across lush meadows – about 800 metres or 15 minutes walk. Return the same way to the footbridge.

Cross the bridge, itself a good viewpoint up the dale, with the massive shape of Kisdon dominating the view to the left, a glacially carved hill isolated between old and new river valleys. Turn sharp right along the well waymarked path through the edge of the wood, which soon crosses meadows and stiles below Ramps Holme Farm. Follow the main path, fairly clear on the ground, across fields, gradually edging towards the river. A lovely riverside

path, including a recently built section around a badly eroded slope below woodland, eventually emerges at Ivelet Bridge, a beautifully arched packhorse bridge. This was on the old Corpse Road from Upper Swaledale, used in medieval times when the only consecrated ground in the dale was at Grinton church. There is still a stone by the bridge on which coffin bearers rested the heavy coffin-baskets. The river here is reputedly a good place to see kingfishers.

Follow the lane to Ivelet, turning right by the estate office to locate a well signposted path across the little gill behind the hamlet. This leads to a lovely path across sloping meadows and past old barns, with magnificent views both up and down the valley. Where the path forks above the river, take the path, clearly visible on the left, which crosses a series of fields to emerge at Gunnerside with its welcoming pub and café. The bus stop back to Reeth and Richmond is just before the bridge.

From the King's Head Inn in Gunnerside walk up the road towards Reeth for 120 metres to where, on the left, a gated road climbs steeply away from the village. Go through the gate but after a few metres at the first hairpin bend take the narrow enclosed track straight ahead, which climbs sharply above the fields and wooded site of Stanley Quarry with its ruined cottages, a small interpretive panel relating their history. As the old lane turns sharp left towards Heights Farm, go across the stile in the wall corner to follow a path along the wall side, over more stiles leading into and through Rowleth Wood, a lovely semi-natural woodland now being replanted. Keep to the waymarked path, broadly in the same direction, losing height slightly before emerging in open pasture, through more stiles, following the hillside as it curves towards Smarber Farm above.

Follow the wall side to the farm and go through the gap, left, past the old barn and new

A characteristic small barn and view across the dale near Rowleth.

agricultural building in front of the farm. Keep on the other side of the wall to a pedestrian gate leading to a path that bears right (not clear on the ground) across a shallow gill with a tiny stream. Cross, following the grassy track ahead which swings down the hillside, but soon leaving it to bear right diagonally down open pasture, heading for the gate in the wall below that indicates the convergence of two footpaths. From this gate, keep straight across the small enclosure towards the woodland where, alongside the wall on the right, you will see a narrow, earth track following the wall downhill. As the main road comes into view, follow the branching track left down to the road. Cross to the triangle of grass, which you can also cross to reach the tarmac lane to Isles Bridge.

Low Lane – an ancient road that forms a lovely walking route along the southern side of the dale.

Left at the junction along the cul-de-sac lane to Low Houses, from where Low Lane, a lovely unsurfaced track, curves along the valley opposite Low Row and Feetham, eventually emerging at Low Whita, south of How Hill, an ancient hill settlement. Keep the same direction, past the junction with Scabba Wath Bridge, climbing steadily eventually to cross the cattle grid and enter open moorland on the left. Where the wall on the left bears away from the road, take the path alongside, which descends towards the river, soon joining the bridleway north of Stubbin Farm, through gates and stiles. This joins a riverside path indicated by stiles (not on all current maps), which takes walkers directly to the newly restored footbridge over the Swale, a bridge destroyed by floods in the late 1990s but rebuilt in 2004 as a flagship Yorkshire Dales Millennium Trust Project.

Cross the bridge, keeping to the main path half right as it climbs towards Reeth, soon joining an enclosed way up to a junction. Right here to the next cross roads, a choice of ways leading into Reeth with its busy village green and excellent choice of cafes, inns and shops, not forgetting the village bakery with homemade bread and cakes where you can buy the superb locally-made Swaledale cheese.

Marrick Priory and Willance's Leap

REETH TO RICHMOND

This walk proves that the lower part of Swaledale is no less spectacular that the upper part of the valley in terms of open views and dramatic landscape features, though more thickly wooded. The route utilises meandering field paths across meadows (please walk single file) but also ancient tracks such as the medieval Nuns' Steps from Marrick Priory, culminating in a spectacular climax along the length of Whitcliffe Scar into Richmond. Wainwright's popular Coast to Coast Path is followed for part of the way, but with some different sections to avoid tarmac and to enjoy even better views.

Route

From Reeth Green head for the old stone pump at the top end of the green, following the lane to the right between cottages, going right again, down to Arkle Guest House. Keep right, alongside the little Arkle Beck into what seems to be a riverside garden, but is also the start of the beckside walk behind the village that emerges underneath and to the far side of Reeth Bridge.

Cross the bridge and at the first corner left take the most southerly of two paths which heads due east over stiles to High Fremington. Follow the lane through the village where slightly to the left the path continues in front of cottages, crossing fields generally by stiles with small pedestrian gates to meet the Marske road west of Fremington. Turn right down to the road junction, and left along the narrow tarmac lane towards Marrick Priory.

To avoid a mile of tarmac, take the step stile reached 50 metres on the left, which leads to a lovely field path, roughly parallel to the road but with better views. It climbs slightly left towards the wire fence above left, where, about half way along and above the field corner, a stile can be found. The path is more or less in a straight line from here, mainly marked by stiles, and is faintly visible across the meadows as the tower of Marrick Priory comes into view.

The path joins the lane at the farm just below the Priory, the subject of a famous

---

FACT FILE

Distance: 12.5 miles (20 kilometres).

Maps: Harvey Dales North (part); OS Explorer OL30, 304.

Terrain: A moderately strenuous walk, undulating throughout, with at least three fairly steep climbs. Mainly field paths and tracks.

Refreshments and accommodation: Café, pubs, B&Bs in Reeth, Youth Hostel at Grinton; no facilities in Marske or Marrick (though some farms on Coast to Coast route offer drinks and light snacks). Choice of cafes, pubs, B&Bs in Richmond.

Toilets: Reeth, Round Howe picnic site, Richmond.

Transport: Outward: Bus 27, 28, X26, X27 from Darlington to Richmond, then 30 to Reeth (on Sundays 830 runs direct from Darlington). Return: 27, 28, X26, X27.

Stage point: Marrick 7 miles – 11km, then 1 mile or 1.6km walk by lane and field path to Downholme Bridge, for return service 30 or 159 to Richmond.

Drivers: Park Richmond and take bus 30 to Reeth.

Swaledale painting and engraving by JMW Turner. A former Benedictine nunnery founded in the twelfth century, it is now converted into a residential youth centre.

A short distance east of the Priory a path crosses to Steps Wood. This is the celebrated Nuns' Causey, a beautiful flagged medieval causeway that climbs steeply through Steps Wood, flanked by wild flowers, eventually following the wall by pastures and entering Marrick village.

The obvious direct track east of the village is not a right of way. Walkers following what is now the Coast to Coast path must loop to the south along the lane around and past the old school house to pick up the path to Hollin Farm, going across several small enclosures and over stiles before entering open pasture. Steady use by Coast to Coast walkers is making this an easy path to follow in what would otherwise be

Marrick Priory, once a Benedictine nunnery and now a youth centre, was immortalised as a romantic ruin in a famous watercolour by Turner.

tricky terrain. It soon crosses the track to Nun Cote Nook (refreshments) before descending North Gill past Ellers, good waymarking and the path on the ground clearly indicating the way uphill to Hollins Farm. The route is to the west of the farm, with a stile in the corner of the wood reached by turning half right once beyond the farm track. The next stile is in the top left-hand corner of a long field, bearing right over a second stile and diagonally over the next field down to Hardstiles Top.

To cut out road walking, leave the Coast to Coast, going left along the lane for 120 metres to a gate where a path heads due northwards

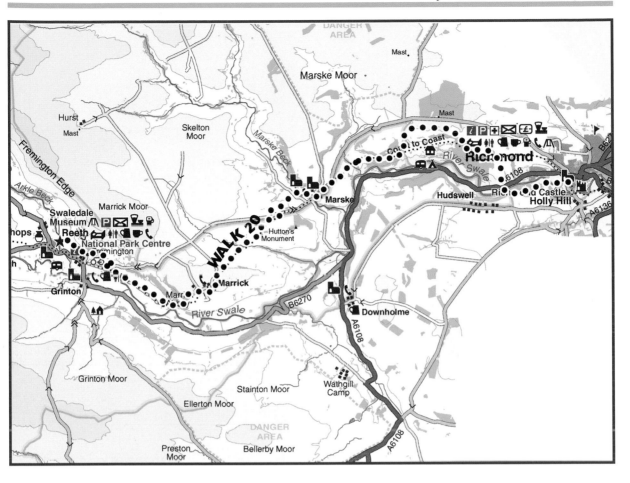

down the field to another stile in the corner. Go directly downhill heading for a small house in Skelton Lane below. To the left of this house is a stile (signed) leading to the path down to Pillmire Bridge, a lovely old stone structure. Note the old wooden waterwheel still in situ close by. Follow the path downstream along-side Marske Beck, which emerges at steps onto Marske Bridge. Turn left into the village.

You are back on the Coast to Coast path. Follow the lane for some 400 metres to where, after it begins to descend, a stile and signpost indicate the path crossing more fields. It descends to a stream and footbridge in a side valley, and a steep climb up the hillside towards Applegarth ahead – a white cairn indicting your destination

The cairn is on a level track, which offers temporary respite as you head towards West Applegarth Farm, again with fine views along the dale. About 50 metres beyond West Applegarth, opposite a ruined barn, look for a blue metal gate on the left. This is the start of a path, which bears right, above a fence, then left again across Salmon Gill, climbing through scrubby woodland over the shoulder of the hill before descending to join the tarmac farm road through Deepdale.

Climb steadily up this steep, narrow pass. At the road summit just before the junction with the Marske road, turn sharp right before the telephone mast on a rocky bluff. This joins the path to the right, along and around Whitcliffe Scar, a magnificent, continuous panoramic viewpoint looking across a thickly wooded landscape, culminating in Willance's Leap. The curious twin memorials commemorate an event in 1606 when Robert Willance, a wealthy Richmond draper's son out hunting on a win-ter's day, became lost in thick fog and mistak-

(Left) *Willance's Monument.*
(Right) *Bargate, the traditional entry point for pedestrians through Richmond's great defensive walls, forms an appropriate ending for those traversing the green networks of the Yorkshire Dales.*

enly galloped his horse over the edge of the cliff. The horse, terrified, took three great leaps, the third into the abyss, falling two hundred feet and killing itself but leaving the rider miraculously with only a broken leg.

It is a superb viewpoint and suitable climax to the walk. The route follows the cliff edge. Keep ahead over stiles and, where the path opens out into pasture, keep to the left of gorse buses ahead. Where a crossing wall comes into view, the path turns sharp right downhill heading towards High Leases Farm. Turn left at the farm, past Whitecliffe Farm, just beyond which – at the Richmond signs – there is a seat and

quotation from Wainwright himself, extolling the fine view across Richmond town.

Take the next track, right, Green Lane, past Low Leases Farm, to a T-junction. Left to Reeth Road. Cross to where a sign indicates the path through the woods to Round Howe picnic site. Cross the footbridge to the National Trust estate, turning left along the riverside path to Billy Bank Wood. Follow the main path as it climbs through lovely woodlands, above cliffs, to Richmond Bridge. Cross, taking the paved way on the right, Bargate, into the town centre.

Richmond has its castle high on a rocky crag above the River Swale, overlooking its busy market place, pubs, cafes, museums, its medieval lanes or wynds and huddle of seventeenth and eighteenth century cottages. Together with its elegant Georgian terraces and unique Georgian Theatre, they form what is simply one of the loveliest towns in the North of England and somewhere well worth spending time, preferably at least one night.

Index

Addingham 25
Addingham Moorside 25
Apedale 96
Arncliffe 69
Askrigg 100
Aysgarth 75

Bainbridge 55
Bell Busk 59
Blazefield 43
Blubberhouses 40
Bolton Castle 96, 101
Bordley 64
Brimham Rocks 44
Buckden 53, 70
Buckden Pike 72
Burley Woodhead 23
Butter Haw 32
Butterton Bridge 46
Bycliffe 49

Carperby 101
Castle Bolton 102
Cauldron Force 74
Chevin 22?
Conistone 48
Cotterdale 88
Cotter End 88
Cracoe 32
Craven Way 82
Crummackdale 78

Dent 83
Denton Moor 27
Dob Park Bridge 39

Elbolton 33

Fairy Dell 27
Feizor 77
Fewston Reservoir 40
Flasby 31

Fountains Abbey 47

Gargrave 58
Garsdale 84, 91
Glasshouses 42
Gordale Scar 64
Gouthwaite Reservoir 51
Grassington 33, 34, 65
Greenhow 37
Grimwith Reservoir 35
Grinton 97
Grinton Smelt Mill 97
Grisedale 84
Guise Cliffe 42
Gunnerside 104

Hardraw Force 88
Harlow Carr 29
Harrogate 29
Haveragh Park 29
Hawes 56, 88, 98
Hebden Gill 35
Hellifield 60, 66
High Fremington 107
High Way 90

Ilkley 25, 26
Ingleborough 78
Ingleton 79, 80
Ivelet Bridge 104

Janet's Foss 64
John o' Gaunt's Reservoir 29

Keld 103
Kettlewell 69, 71
Kilnsey 48
Kirkby Malham 67
Kirkby Stephen 87, 93
Kirk Sink 59
Kisdon 103

Lacon Cross 46
Lammerside Castle 93
Leathley 38
Leyburn 94
Lindley Wood Reservoir 39?
Linton Falls 33, 65
Lippersley Pike 28
Litherskew 100
Little Fell 86
Litton 70
Lunds 91

Malham 63, 68
Malham Cove 68
Malham Tarn 68
Marrick 108
Marrick Priory 108
Marske 109
Menston 23
Middlesmoor 51
Middleton 26
Mill Gill Force 100
Mossdale 49
Mossy Moor Reservoir 35
Muker 104

Nateby 93
Newbiggin 101
Nun's Causey 108

Otley 21, 38
Otterburn 59, 66

Pateley Bridge 37, 42, 43, 52
Pecca Falls 80
Pendragon Castle 93
Preston-under-Scar 95

Ramsgill 51
Redmire 96, 102
Reeth 97, 106, 107
Richmond 110

Ripon 47
Rombald's Moor 23
Rowleth Wood 105
Rylstone 32

Sandy Gate 48
Scaleber Force 60
Sedbusk 56, 98
Semerwater 54
Settle 60, 61, 76
Sharp Haw 31
Skelterton 32
Skenrith 86
Skipton 25, 30, 57

Stackhouse 76
Stake Pass 53
Stalling Busk 54
Starbotton 71
Studley Roger 47
Studley Royal 47
Stump Cross Caverns 36
Swarth Fell 85
Swinsty Hall 28
Swinsty Reservoir 28, 39

Thornton Force 80
Thorpe 33
Threapland 32

Threshfield 65
Thruscross Reservoir 40
Timble 28

Walden 73
Wath 52
Weets Cross 64
West Burton 74
Wharfe 78
Wharton Hall 93
Whernside 81
Whitcliffe Scar 109
Wild Boar Fell 85

Mossy track near Kisdon, Upper Swaledale (Walk 19)